Resonate

Resonate

How to Preach
for Deep Connection

LISA WASHINGTON LAMB

Foreword by Mark A. Labberton

CASCADE *Books* • Eugene, Oregon

RESONATE
How to Preach for Deep Connection

Copyright © 2022 Lisa Washington Lamb. All rights reserved. Except for brief quotations in critical publications or reviews, no part of this book may be reproduced in any manner without prior written permission from the publisher. Write: Permissions, Wipf and Stock Publishers, 199 W. 8th Ave., Suite 3, Eugene, OR 97401.

Cascade Books
An Imprint of Wipf and Stock Publishers
199 W. 8th Ave., Suite 3
Eugene, OR 97401

www.wipfandstock.com

PAPERBACK ISBN: 978-1-6667-3557-4
HARDCOVER ISBN: 978-1-6667-9278-2
EBOOK ISBN: 978-1-6667-9279-9

Cataloguing-in-Publication data:

Names: Lamb, Lisa Washington. | Foreword by Mark A. Labberton.

Title: Resonate : how to preach for deep connection / Lisa Washington Lamb; Mark A. Labberton, foreword.

Description: Eugene, OR: Cascade Books, 2022 | Includes bibliographical references.

Identifiers: ISBN 978-1-6667-3557-4 (paperback) | ISBN 978-1-6667-9278-2 (hardcover) | ISBN 978-1-6667-9279-9 (ebook)

Subjects: LCSH: Preaching. | Pastoral theology.

Classification: BV4211.3 L30 2022 (print) | BV4211.3 (ebook)

To all who are enduring challenging seasons and still striving to communicate God's good news with excellence and love.

Table of Contents

Foreword ix

Acknowledgments xiii

Introduction xv

1. Preacher as Witness and Host:
   The Power of First-Person Speech 1

2. Preacher as Shepherd:
   The Promise of Second-Person Speech 17

3. Preacher as Proclaimer:
   Declaring God's Goodness with Third-Person-Singular Verbs 28

4. Preacher as Sage:
   Teaching Wisdom with Third-Person-Plural Verbs 41

5. Preacher as Storyteller:
   Fueling Faith by Narrating the Past 56

6. Preacher as Priest:
   Discerning the Work of God in the Present 70

7. Preacher as Visionary Prophet:
   Walking into the Future with Hope 85

8. Preacher as Leader:
   Choosing and Using Modes of Influence 101

TABLE OF CONTENTS

9   Preacher as Catalyst:
Sparking Transformation in the Active and Passive Voice 117

Conclusion 133

Bibliography 137

Foreword

by MARK LABBERTON

THE CELLIST OF SARAJEVO sat amidst the ruins of war, and for twenty-two days in 1992 played with exquisite beauty and anguish to honor each of the twenty-two people killed while standing in line for bread. The cultural and musical history that preceded the horrors of this war, the chaotic destruction that set this tragic scene—and now, the lone, technical, soulful artist sat amid it all—day after day, and played the notes and the beauty of profound music expressing the heartbreak and hope of human life. Musical resonance like this may be the hallmark of human communion and communication. The people of Sarajevo, and of the world, resonated with the tears, the pain, the longing, and the hope of such an act.

It is said of music that the notes set the musical stage but it's the overtones that fill the heart. The overtones of Sarajevo were thick. Resonance carries a message to the heart and mind, to the individual and the community. It's the vibrations of harmony and dissonance that convey what we can then trust enough to receive its message into our souls. Communication with resonance fosters trust, and trust is the prerequisite to communion.

Lisa Lamb draws us here into the realization of what it takes for the verbal and emotional resonance of preaching to do this very work. Words are our verbal notes, drawn from the deep well of Scripture, formed by millennial practices of the people of God, that now land in the raw landscape of our lives so we can hear to our core the good news of God's love and justice in Jesus Christ, our enduring "cellist of Sarajevo." When words—especially verbs—set the stage, and when those words are well-played, faith can grow, even soar with gospel transformation.

Foreword

All of this is so much easier said than done. The acoustics of musical connectivity and virtuosity flows from the rich blend of art and of science. That is, the construction of the cello's design, wood, glue, resins, and so on, sets up the possibilities for sonatas to remake our lives. All of this is far from simple, but when it happens it can seem natural and obvious. The resonance grips and fills us.

Week by week the preacher prepares to speak the word of God to the people of God. The gift of Holy Scripture, its witness to the revelation of God as Creator, Redeemer, and Sustainer, in the complex history of Israel, through the birth and growth of the church in all its manifestations, and the continuing contextualization across time and geographies, cultures, and surrounding realities, all precede and surround the preacher now standing in the pulpit.

The cellist of Sarajevo didn't just grab a cello and play random notes. Instead, it was the composer, the instrument maker, the music teacher, the hours and hours of solitary technical and musical skill building and artistic maturing that preceded the unexpected moment—the offering heard around the world. What the cellist is doing is resonant with the materials but now he is making the music resonant with the audience. The practice honed the technique that released the artistry and brought the audience to feel that in the very midst of death there was life.

The preacher likewise deploys the rigors of scriptural text, history, and interpretation, the discernment of prayer, listening, spiritual reflection, intuition, and choosing language to convey and resonate in love with the congregation so their lives resonate with the One who makes all things new. It is the cumulation and practice of the biblical, personal, liturgical, resonant love that makes the words of the preacher the words of Life.

Dr. Lamb makes here such a compelling case that within the preacher and the sermon lies one of the most important, if underappreciated, ingredients for deepest resonance: verbs. No doubt all the other elements contribute to strong preaching, but verbs resonate with our being and our doing in the presence of the Living God. Faith is a verb. Love is a verb. Obedience is a verb. Confession and lament are verbs. Thanks, praise, serve, and sacrifice—all verbs.

What Lamb makes clear is that the vocation of preaching is about all that precedes entering the pulpit, as much as it is about what happens once the preacher is in it. She explains why and how, by the Holy Spirit, seeking deep resonance makes the Word come alive—in Sarajevo or wherever

Foreword

the good news sounds. Learn from her some of the lessons that help us be prepared for Ordinary Time, for Advent, Lent, or Pentecost, in seasons of devastation, of joy, and every other day or time, so the Word of Life may land with transformative power.

Acknowledgments

I AM SO THANKFUL to the many friends and family members who encouraged me in the process of bringing this book from idea to finished book. I am thankful to Marguerite Shuster, Clayton Schmit, and David T. Lamb, who read early chapters with interest and insight. Dorothy Littell Greco brought pastoral wisdom and valiantly wrested many a mixed metaphor from the text. I am grateful to John Witchger, Maria Teresa Gaston, and Nancy Washington for reading portions of the book with enthusiasm. Thanks as well to many colleagues at Fuller Theological Seminary and St. Paul's Theological College, Malaysia for their friendship and partnership. In particular, Amos Yong, Mark Labberton, Joel Green, and Ahmi Lee championed the book early on. Many thanks to my children, Becca and Avery Davis Lamb and Mark and Leslie Lamb for their encouragement along the way. I have been sustained by rich friendships throughout the pandemic season in which this book was written, including Beth and Bob Kinsey, Lauri Dennis, Sherri and Dustin Ellington, Mark and Gayll Phifer-Houseman, Tim and Jennie Genske, and Jeff and Sharon Bjork. Finally, I'm grateful beyond words for my husband, Rich Lamb, who never flags as an advocate, friend, partner, and reliable source of endless mirth.

Introduction

It was a nerve-wracking preaching moment. I was auditioning for a job as I preached, though few people in the church that day knew that. The search committee was divided, so their members would be listening for vastly different things. A well-meaning friend said, "You have to knock it out of the park!" Though I was tempted to try to dazzle them, I chose instead to bring a simple, faithful word that flowed from the passage of Scripture. Afterward, an older man approached me. He was a Bible scholar who was steeped like tea in its words. He smiled affectionately and slowly spoke six words. "*Your sermon resonated with the text.*" I probably heard other kind words that day; I do not remember them. His words landed deep in my spirit as a blessing and a gift. They gave me a goal I pursue every time I preach—resonance.

When two musical notes vibrate together pleasingly, their resonance draws out the beauty of each note and delights our ears. When companions are wholly at ease with each other, conversing with deep trust and affection, we say they have resonance. The more poetic among us might say their "heartstrings" resonate. When a wise friend speaks back to you—with utmost empathy and insight—the pain you just disjointedly narrated, you say, "Yes! That resonates."

When we preach, we aim to sound a true note that echoes faithfully with Scripture's first words, enlivening the hearts of our listeners, connecting them with God as it names their pain and awakening hope as it sounds new possibilities. We dare to voice an authentic note that exposes our own struggle, letting that link us to the suffering of our listeners. But how can we know what will hit home and what will fall flat?

The question haunts us every Saturday night for those of us who preach weekly. "Does it resonate? Will it connect?" We sweated over the sermon, pressing the words out of our keyboards like the last slow steps of

Introduction

an uphill run. We wrestled hard with our Scripture text, coaxing it to speak its truth so we could convey that to our listeners. We attempted a clear, logical flow, a catchy introduction, and a compelling conclusion, all toward the goal of saying something true and beautiful about the gospel to people we love. It *seems* finished—we certainly feel done with working on it! But could it be missing a dimension that would let it land with transforming impact? We sigh. "How can I tell?" It seems impossible to know with any certainty, like guessing the perpetrator in a murder mystery when we are three chapters into it.

But might there be telltale clues in plain sight if we only had the right magnifying glass with which to see them? On one level, preaching is indeed a mysterious endeavor. We never know what will hit and what will miss. This uncertainty makes us feel vulnerable, and rightly so. Our incapacity to "make something happen" when we preach turns us to God in humble and prayerful dependence. The Holy Spirit is the One who empowers our words and moves in the minds and hearts of listeners. Lydia's experience is paradigmatic for all hearers: "*The Lord* opened her heart to respond to Paul's message" (Acts 16:14). This truth both thrills and frustrates every pastor every Sunday. One week, it seems clear from listeners' feedback that the sermon spoke powerfully. Why? "It's a mystery," we say to ourselves. The following week, all indications are that the sermon we felt just as confident about flopped. Fizzled. Fell short. Why? "It's a mystery."

This response can seem to be a faithful, leave-it-to-the-Lord approach. And it is, in part. But what if there were a way to test a sermon's strength—its potential to resonate—before we flung it out there, the way we test a ship for seaworthiness before we unleash it to cross a turbulent sea? Can we foresee what by God's grace will touch and energize a community and what will miss them entirely? I believe there is such a way. I want to teach you a simple, practical method of testing the crucial connection points that too often go missing in our preaching. We'll get to that method shortly; first, let's notice how preaching is changing and why making a connection is so essential today.

Resonance arguably happens best in person and in real time. The global pandemic we have endured has played with our conceptions of what it means to be "in person," as presence has been mediated through screens. Pastors gamely added the verb "pivot" to their vocabulary and set to work recording, editing, and uploading content, Zooming, streaming live, or trying various hybrid combinations. Many things went surprisingly well. But

Introduction

every preacher has struggled with *presence* and *connection*. We have felt the lack or reduction of it as an aching void.

If we did not know it before, we learned at a visceral level that *being there* and *being with* matter immensely to us humans. From the gripping photos of elderly couples smooching through glass to the poignant air hugs we gave old friends out on their lawns to the silly hearts my son and daughter-in-law and I make with our arms as we say goodbye across thousands of miles, we have seen that we are wired to connect with others. And we are also wired to respond together to good news. At its essence, the definition of a preacher is one who brings good news from God's Word to persons they love.

The sermon is not fading in relevance or importance, much as some church pundits lament—and a few celebrate—its demise. However, its shape and the venues in which it happens may morph dramatically. If the church is to flourish in the coming decades, I predict that it will need many, many more people who conceive of themselves as preachers, at least in part. Preaching itself will be redefined and reinvigorated. As we feel our way forward, navigating new spaces and modes of coming together as faith communities, be assured that, whether at a distance or in person, preaching will continue to be one of a pastoral leader's most potent tools of influence. More than ever, it will matter that we see it as a way of intentionally *being present with* the people we love and lead. We are hungry to connect.

As you seek to preach sermons that rebuild those bonds, I invite you to pay attention to your *verbs*. The verbs tell the story every time. If you look closely, they even have stories to tell about you. The verb forms you use and the ones you avoid may reveal a deep and persistent weariness, a deficit of hope, or a fraying of confidence in your capacity to lead as you emerge from this hard season. You are on a journey with your congregation, and your sermons are one indicator of where you are, what fuel or rest you need, and when a course correction may be needed. Pay attention.

Harnessing the power of the full range of verb forms can spark moments of deep resonance—uniting listeners to God and each other and linking preachers with listeners. Conversely, our overuse or neglect of certain verb forms can be the source of a tragic failure to connect. To understand how that works, we will need to get under the hood of the language engine ever so briefly and pick apart the forms of verbs. That sounds a bit daunting—some of us barely remember words like *subjunctive* from school.

Introduction

Let me share the moment I came to love conjugating (labeling the parts of) verbs.

My earnest high school Latin teacher strode up and down our rows of desks, arms flapping like a crazed cheerleader, coaxing us to shout out the categories of the verbs on the board. I wondered, "Why is she so excited about this?" At first, it felt tedious, then oddly satisfying, then weirdly exhilarating. As we dissected those ancient verbs, we were solving a mystery, dusting for the fingerprints, the intent, and motives of long-dead Roman authors. We labeled every verb with our secret-spy-club code: *Person. Number. Tense. Mode. Voice.* Above each verb, we jotted esoteric labels like 3P-Pl-F-I-A (third-person plural, future tense, indicative mode, active voice), deciphering until the sentences made sense. (We had to do some crazy stuff to the nouns, too—we will decline to do that here.) The verb categories became familiar friends like they never had in English classes. Our own language is so intuitive that we sometimes only see its internal logic when cracking the code of another one. With my decoder ring in hand, I could tackle whatever messy sentences ancient authors like Livy or Catullus threw my way.

As a preaching professor, I have listened to thousands of sermons. As a pastor, I have preached my share. When I tease out the flat sides and the disconnects in otherwise strong sermons, I find myself using the code of the verb forms. They stand out to me for a good reason. Preaching is a dynamic speech act. It trades in verbs as it promises, declares, warns, and inspires. It plays furtively with tense and time, asserting that events from centuries ago carry meaning for today. It claims that events yet to happen can exert shaping force on us this week. It nimbly shifts mode as it describes, invites, and even commands. It names the passive and active dimensions of transformation into the image of Jesus Christ.

Preaching asserts a lively God who is active in the world and the heart of every listener. So, it makes sense that we attend to language's sprightliest part of speech, the verb. Sermons do not just want to look pretty on a page or be doctrinally precise; they want to *do* something—to catalyze transformation. Verbs are literally where the action is, and how we use, neglect, or misuse them reveals our theology, heart, and capacity to be present with our listeners. Well chosen verbs connect us with our listeners, and poorly chosen ones alienate us from them. Dexterous verb-craft lets us navigate four essential aspects of pastoral leadership:

Introduction

Identity and Presence: We pay attention to the dominant *person* of our verbs as their use or absence reveals whether we are present with our people and offering ourselves to them.

Marking Time: A pastoral leader keeps time for the church, sounding the past, present, and future *tense* to enable listeners to look back, around, and ahead together.[1]

Influence: A verb's *mode* gives us tools of influence—we describe reality, imagine change, and compel listeners to respond.

Transformation: We will designate the active and passive *voice* as the realm where we consider the interplay of our human effort and God's work in change processes. We welcome and receive the transformative work of the Holy Spirit to bring about what we never could accomplish alone, but we also embrace the agency we possess to participate in that work.

Some of us need these broken down a bit more. The concept of verb forms makes more intuitive, immediate sense to native speakers of *inflected* languages.[2] In English, we work our verbs hard. Some languages let their verbs alone, not asking them to do the heavy lifting of encoding oodles of meaning within a single word.[3] Inflected languages are in no way "superior" to non-inflected ones, but they give us a vocabulary for analyzing what a verb is up to in a sentence. If your first language is not an inflected one, or if you (understandably) fell asleep in grammar class, here is a quick review. When we analyze a verb, we ask questions about:

Person[4]
    First Person: "I thirst."
    Second Person: "You are the light of the world."
    Third Person: "He, too, is a son of Abraham."

---

1. Lundblad develops the concept of sermons marking time in her book, *Marking Time*.

2. An inflected language changes the form or ending of some words when the way in which they are used in sentences changes.

3. For example, in Malay, *makan* means eat, ate, or will eat, and I, we, or they eat, as other markers of time and person are added around it.

4. Here we are folding in the category of *Number*, whether a verb is singular or plural.

Introduction

Tense[5]

Past: "I found my lost sheep."

Future: "You will deny me three times."

Present: "It is finished."

Mode[6]

Indicative Mode describes reality: "Jesus Christ offers us grace."

Imperative Mode commands: "Receive the grace of Christ today!"

Subjunctive Mode imagines: "What if we *were to* let Jesus' grace transform us?"

Voice

Active Voice: The subject *does* the action. "They hear the word with joy."

Passive Voice: The subject *receives* the action. "Her sins are forgiven."

That's it. You will do essentially everything you do in a sermon with these eleven verbal forms. Like the tools in a tool kit, each does a few specific tasks well and fails when attempting to do others. Preachers who learn this paradigm will know how and when to activate each verbal form. They will be able to look at a sermon and readily notice which ones are weak or altogether missing and what that will mean for the sermon's tone and reach. Of course, not every sermon needs to employ every form, but it does need to answer why not and avoid overreliance on any one mode.

This book is not about concocting the perfect verbal blend, cunningly calculated to strum listeners' heartstrings. Of course, we want our preaching to touch hearts, but only in the service of letting God transform those hearts, not for some feel-good result that earns us accolades. Nor is this book primarily about how to write better. You will not hear me counseling you to *use more active verbs*—the drumbeat of every writing improvement blog. It is excellent advice. It should be endeavored. (Just kidding.) That is not this book's topic. Instead, the verb forms are, in part, metaphors for dimensions within preaching, starting points for conversations about frequently missed opportunities for resonance. For example, in this book, the active and passive voice becomes a code for exploring the language we use to study human and divine agency and participation in the transformation

---

5. Many languages have a few variations within the past tense, such as perfect or imperfect, but we will keep it simple.

6. Mode is sometimes referred to as *mood*, but I find this confuses listeners who (rightly) think of moods as emotional states.

Introduction

process, even though the process does not align precisely with that grammatical form.

Any paradigm risks rigidity or a focus on mechanically ticking boxes. My goal is not that you work your way through this paradigm as a perfunctory checklist each week, but instead that it would drive you to a deeper pursuit of God-honoring excellence in your proclamation, rooted in love for the people who listen. I hope this process will compel you to become wiser and more joyful as you live into your vocation to speak good news in a new season where we all desperately need to hear it. That, in turn, will foster a more profound sense of presence and connection with the people you love. I believe that honors and delights the heart of God.

1

Preacher as Witness and Host

The Power of First-Person Speech

> "If preachers decide to preach about hope,
> let them preach out of what they themselves hope for."
> —FREDERICK BUECHNER

IT CAN SEEM IRREVERENT to start our verb-craft survey with ourselves. Shouldn't we start with God or with Scripture?[1] We begin here in part because every verb conjugation chart begins here.[2] But we also do so because of the inevitably personal and embodied nature of preaching. This chapter looks at how we use first-person-singular speech to bring ourselves as witnesses and how we use first-person plural ("we" language) to lead as hosts who welcome every listener to feast upon the word.

---

1. I do not present these elements in an order to suggest that we should introduce them in that order within a sermon. Andy Stanley argues for sermons generally following a specific order of segments, and his order in fact begins here, with a section revealing the preacher's own questions, problems, or needs. Stanley's model has much to commend it (and some problematic aspects as well), but this book does not advocate a specific pattern so much as that we pay attention to excesses and gaps in our preaching. Stanley and Jones, *Communicating for a Change*, chapter 13.

2. I also acknowledge that some sermon forms follow a different overall design, one in which pronouns play a different role. For instance, a narrative sermon may use the first person to narrate from the perspective of a character.

First-Person Singular: The Witness

I was not thrilled to tell the story of the C-minus I received on a midterm in my first semester of seminary when I preached in chapel at that same school years later. In my defense, there was a brutal set of extenuating circumstances the week before the midterm. Still, it did not exactly portray me as a stellar scholar to the fellow faculty who would be present. But the story kept pawing at me like a puppy begging to go out. It was a perfect fit for the theme of resilience after failure in my Scripture passage, and I could not shake the sense that it would encourage the students who heard it. Reluctantly, I threw it in. I had not predicted how much it would spark a connection between my students and me, a former fellow struggling student. That moment let me speak credible and convincing words of hope straight into their hearts as their midterms were fast approaching. This chapter will dive into the power of speaking from the first-person singular and plural—how sentences or phrases that begin with *I* allow us to witness and ones that begin with *We* help us to welcome and host those who gather to hear the word with us.

There is no escaping that preaching puts *you*, the preacher, near the center of the endeavor. Writers can fling their creations into the world from the safety of their homes and even write under cover of pseudonyms if they desire. Actors risk in ways that are more like preachers in that they place their bodies on a stage before onlookers. But their words are not their own, and we (hopefully) do not judge the likability of actors based on the characters they enact.

Preachers pull from the scariest bits of both those endeavors. They write their own content (in response to the words of Scripture), and then they take a deep breath, get up in front, and perform it. Here, I use the word *perform* in its best sense—not putting on a show merely for applause but drawing from its root meaning of *giving shape* to something, bringing an idea to tangible expression, or a goal to completion. A contractor and construction crew perform an architect's plans, just as a conductor and orchestra perform a composer's score. Performing requires faithful attention to the designer's intent. It is a vulnerable and strenuous endeavor, without which blueprints are just rolls of paper, and sermons are just words, with no transformative power.

Preaching starts with brave and sometimes trembling individuals standing up to voice their belief, struggle, and delight. And this is by *design*. God has chosen human vulnerability as the starting point for the

Preacher as Witness and Host

God-with-us endeavor of preaching. As Barbara Brown Taylor puts it, "By choosing Christ to flesh out the word, God made a lasting decision in favor of incarnation. Those of us who are his body in the world need not shy away from the fact that our own flesh and blood continue to be where the word of God is made known."[3]

Taylor's words are equal parts exhilarating and terrifying. The personal element in preaching can go wrong fast in seventeen ways. The risks abound—from feeding narcissism to breeding preachers who compose sermons calculated entirely to please. But we cannot run from bringing ourselves to preaching in a misguided effort to manage the risks. I recall as a child hearing a preacher say, in response to being praised after a service, "That wasn't me up there." Since he sat in a spot hidden from view before he preached, my overactive childhood imagination pictured a Spirit-pastor body swap that went on back there just before he stood up. His words reflected a well-intended effort at humility, but they left me genuinely confused.

The presence of the preacher has always been tricky. For centuries, the church has solved the perceived problem by advising preachers to exit their sermons as much as possible. "Hide yourself behind the cross" seems like noble and humble advice. But it is theologically and psychologically suspect and frankly sounds a little creepy, like my childhood ghost-pastor. The optimal sermon becomes one where the preacher has managed to disappear entirely, much like the disappearing act of the human Jesus in one of the heresies of the early church.[4]

The danger is subtle yet runs deep. If we assert that God magically takes the wheel, preachers become unassailable, far above challenge and correction. It is a fiction that is psychologically untenable for listeners or preachers. When you preach, wholeheartedly pray for God to speak through you, but please don't pray to disappear. Instead, pray to be fully present. Let it be your authentic voice that speaks. Dare to bring your body, with all it has endured and enjoyed. Bring us your experience of the piercing presence and the frustrating absence of God. Disappearing acts are not noble. Wholeheartedly offering of yourself is. It is brave to risk embarrassment and shame if you fail, or alienating listeners if you press too hard, and risk judgment if a personal story comes back to bite you in an awkward

---

3. Taylor, *Preaching Life*, 84.

4. Docetism taught that Jesus only appeared to have a real, human body during his life on earth.

elders meeting. Bringing ourselves to the preaching moment is a gift we freely offer. Gift-giving, even among the best of friends, always carries risk. The risk is an inevitable and crucial part of the gift.

How do we bring ourselves more fully to our preaching? Starting at the shallow end of the pool, a simple way to start would be to use a "find and replace" tool to scan for the word "I." How many sentences begin with that word? The results may surprise you. If every third one starts with "I," you are making yourself the star of the show. If none do, you are missing a pivotal pathway to resonance. But a surface-level scan will not tell the whole story. You need to ask what those sentences are doing. What are they revealing, and what are they studiously hiding? Are you intentionally and gladly present, offering your story and faith as a gift? Let me spell out why I believe this is so important. We give our listeners three gifts when we dare to bring ourselves wholeheartedly to our sermons: a shared journey of discovery, and ourselves as trustworthy witnesses and fellow travelers on the path of discipleship.

A Shared Journey of Discovery

As a listener, I love to hear a preacher say, "I was so confused by this passage earlier this week! I wondered why on earth Jesus said these words in this way! But then I started looking at the action going on around his words, and I wondered if that might provide a clue." When preachers do this, they make a familiar text enticingly strange. Well-traveled paths become new territory to explore. Preachers who expose their initial or even ongoing puzzlement with Scripture stand at the trailhead excitedly handing out walking sticks, inviting their listeners to go on the strenuous journey they took with the Scripture this past week. They are comfortable displaying themselves as learners, diligent students of Scripture who did not get it all down pat on the first pass. Augustine did this regularly in his preaching. After pondering sections that confused him in a sermon on the Psalms, he says, "Although we are teachers to you, we are also fellow students with you under that one teacher."[5]

As well as exposing our confusion or initial resistance, we can intentionally expose our love and delight. Here we stand at the trailhead holding out binoculars, urging, "Don't miss the stunning vista up ahead!" That launches people on a different discovery journey—a quest to see the beauty

---

5. Augustine, *Expositions of the Psalms*, Psalm 126.

and goodness of the God that the Scriptures uncover. This practice carries its own type of vulnerability. We worry that we will sound starry-eyed and naïve when we lay bare our childlike love for Jesus Christ. You bet we will. That is built into our job description; we get to be the "holy fools" Paul describes in 1 Corinthians (1:18; 2:18–19) who model simple faith and exuberant delight. When a preacher liberally peppers her sermon with, "I love the way Jesus . . ." or "I am so glad that the psalmist adds the phrase . . ." she is inviting us to share her sheer pleasure in the Scriptures and the God they reveal. She is bringing herself but ultimately pointing to Jesus Christ and his faithfulness.

A Trustworthy Witness

When we offer our confusion and our delight in Scripture, we are better able to shape our sermons as shared journeys of discovery. When we offer our faith and belief in God, we live into the biblical image of the witness, who boldly testifies to what he or she has seen and experienced. Our legal systems place much faith in the testimony of witnesses, which is somewhat surprising given that witnesses may remember poorly. They forget event sequences, conflate separate events, and bring in biases. Yet, in courts around the globe, we count on witnesses to piece together the picture, for they were present at a critical moment. Like Moses turning aside to see why the burning bush was not consumed, they stopped what they were doing long enough to focus on what was happening before them. They took it in and let it affect them. Witnesses caught a glimpse and paid attention. That alone makes them worthy of a hearing.

 A pulpit is thankfully not a witness stand, with an attorney interrogating us while we preach. Church as courtroom is not an attractive or compelling metaphor. Sticking with our journey imagery, a witness is a seasoned traveler on the road of faith formation, a guide who knows from experience what dangers to avoid and what vistas are worth walking extra miles not to miss. We testify to our lived experience of God's faithfulness, Scripture's truth, and what has worked and not worked in our faltering attempts to live out its truths. This strengthens our listeners' belief and trust in the ultimate guide on the journey. It buoys faith within us to hear a credible articulation of another persons' journey to faith or an instance where God intervened. Some listeners arrive at church entirely out of gas, needing to lean into the church's faith, as a preacher gives voice to it. They may even need to let the faith of another carry them for a stretch of the road.

We offer our faith to others because belief engenders belief. To say preachers *model* faith is not to say they must be perfect, model citizens of God's kingdom. Think more of a clay model that forms a template for an ongoing project. It gets the project going and guides it intermittently. Organizational consultants William and Susan Bridges put it this way:

> If you have ever watched people learning to swim, you will remember that critical moment when they pushed off from the edge of the pool and set forth on their own. You may have heard the swim instructor say, "I won't let you sink." Without trust in the teacher, that step toward independence and mastery of a new skill would have been less likely to happen. At that moment, with fear balanced against hope, it is trust that makes the difference. Not yet trusting their own ability to swim, they fall back on trusting the teacher.[6]

As we testify, we enable people to walk from trust in us to trust also in God. You could be that swimming instructor in the realm of faith, one whose trustworthy testimony allows a newcomer to the pool to jump in and discover the grace of Jesus Christ and the joy of following him. When we witness, we strengthen credibility, authenticity, and connection. I love the way preacher Hosanna Wong did this in a sermon on fear. She proclaimed, "Failing has made me bolder. Loss has made me braver. I learned that I could fail and survive. I learned that I could fall and get back up. God rescued me again and again. Now I know how safe I am."[7]

A Fellow Traveler

When we let ourselves show up in our sermons, we offer not only our encounters with Scripture and our faith, but our failings and struggles as vulnerable gifts to our communities. We reveal our unfulfilled longings, fears, and frustrations. As pastor and author Andy Stanley winsomely notes, "I go out of my way to lay my humanity and frailty out on the front of the stage. Doing so tears down walls. Besides, if you preach from weakness,

---

6. Bridges and Bridges, *Managing Transitions*, 119.

7. Wong, "I Will Not Be Afraid," sermon preached at Eastlake Church, Chula Vista, CA, October 9, 2018, https://www.youtube.com/watch?v=QCOpy9h_cao.

you will never run out of material."[8] That endless material includes exposing the ways we struggle to live out the truth or the ways we have received the grace of Jesus, perhaps as glimpsed through a friend's freely offered forgiveness. We share the aching desires that stirred within us as we read of God's kingdom and saw the chasm between our lives and its description of a life well lived. And we testify to how God has graciously met us in our struggles, not necessarily to win for us a triumphant victory, but always to enable us to endure.

Sharing our weakness is more complicated than sharing what we did not at first understand but later came to love about a passage. As we set out to offer our stories, we find ourselves maneuvering a road checkered with potholes. So why do we do it? Because we seek resonance. We sound a note and hope it resonates, that a chord is struck within listeners who feel similar pain, disappointment, or grief, though they may not have yet articulated it. Paul was a passionate practitioner of letting his own life speak. He exposed his various struggles in his letters and narrated his conversion with brutal honesty in the book of Acts. There he confesses his persecution of Christians and testifies to how God met and transformed him.[9]

Barbara Brown Taylor writes about the risks and benefits of personal illustrations. "People may become more interested in what I am up to than in what the text is up to, and that is where it goes awry. But what I mean to be doing is offering my listeners a little chunk of our common humanity, so they can say, 'Oh, you too? What a relief!' The point is for people to see themselves, not me, but sometimes it is safer for them to do that sideways by identifying with me."[10] Our story of failure may provide listeners a chance to reckon with realities they are eagerly avoiding. Such testimony can spark and form faith in listeners. But we will need to steer away from the worst of the potholes. Let me give you five driving tips.

1. *Reckon with the emotive power of your story.* Narrative can carry more power than we estimate, which is not an unalloyed good. Its potency makes it volatile; it can slip away from our grasp. When we tell our stories well, they quickly become the most memorable moments in a sermon. If a story brings the most humorous moment, it will naturally be what surfaces first in memory in the coming week for listeners.

---

8. Stanley and Jones, *Communicating for a Change*, chapter 13.
9. Acts 22:1–21; 24:10–21; 26:2–27.
10. Taylor, "Bothering God," 158.

But if a story elicits the most poignant moment, it will not only be memorable; it may also derail a listener emotionally. For some, that emotional force may simply distract to the point that it overtakes the impact of Scripture and its truths. For others, it may trigger feelings from past trauma. Personal stories can tap a similar memory of fear, pain, or shame in listeners, who may not have expected that pain to be tapped as they took their seats. As the teller of the tale, some details that you feel are crucial may be excessively disturbing to your listeners. Here is where the advice, "Show us your scars, not your wounds," is helpful but does not go quite far enough. It can be counterproductive to share a trauma that has not been significantly healed within you, but even one that is fully processed and healed for *you* may trigger trauma in a listener. Restraint with details will guard against a recklessness that can harm more than help. And be highly restrained with stories about family members. Your child may agree to you sharing a story about them to please you and because they don't feel they possess the agency to say no.

2. *Tether it to the text.* As you reckon with a personal story's power, be sure that you are more interested in what God is up to in your passage than what your own life can teach. Tie your story tightly to the themes of your text. Tethering takes discipline and intentionality, especially for "natural" storytellers. Narratives have inherent value, and in the right setting, extending them can be delightful. If you are a gifted teller of tales, let them spin out unfettered around a campfire or at the family reunion. But in a sermon, stories must be servants to a greater purpose, whether clarifying a truth or positioning that truth to reach the heart. The word *illustration* has its roots in lustrous brightness—the best ones shine a light not on themselves but on the ultimate Subject of our sermon. Tell your story, and then *turn* your story upward.

3. *Know your wingspan.* Acknowledge that not all listeners will relate to your stories. You have a wingspan, a limited range of natural connection points with your congregation. You will naturally connect best with those whose lived experiences are similar, whether due to gender, age, socioeconomic and educational congruence, or personality. Your finitude is an argument for a diverse preaching team. But if you are a solo pastor, you can extend your reach by first getting specific with an event in your life and then broadening. As you craft an illustration from your own life, drill down to the core of the experience you want

to capture and think through what is generalizable about it. Ask yourself, "How could someone who has never experienced this (endured a hailstorm while backpacking, given birth in their car, or lost both parents as a child) still relate to what I felt and learned at that moment? What common longings, fears, and lessons am I appealing to here?" This practice of drilling to bedrock and then broadening to encompass others communicates a humble awareness that our own story is not paradigmatic for the life of every member of our congregation. It does not need to be. We simply need to remember that it is not. Tell your story, and then turn your story outward.

4. *Avoid shrinking the biblical story to the size of yours.* In our attempts to relate to the suffering of a biblical character, we can become guilty of stuffing Scripture's stories into the small stockings of our own misadventures. Old Testament scholar Ellen Davis, writing on how (not) to preach the Psalms, cautions, "In preaching, as in prayer, we should be wary of laying exclusive claim to the psalmist's persistent 'I.' No preacher's life can stretch big enough to fit every psalm, nor can it possibly be interesting enough to warrant such totalitarianism."[11] We may have caught a tiny glimpse of what Joseph felt in that pit when we were trapped in a barn for an hour, but it was not a full grasp, so tell it as a glimpse.

5. *Edit relentlessly.* Assess your story's fit with Scripture and sermon. Does it illuminate or merely relate to the topic? Too often, our thought process goes like this: "This Syrophoenician woman asks for the crumbs from the table. My dog does that, too! Let me talk for a while about my dog." That may delight briefly, but ultimately it merely distracts. It leads people away from Scripture rather than more deeply into it. As engrossing as the tale of your minor car fire last week is, you need to ask how well it resonates with this text and its themes. If it does, tell it. We love a car fire story if everyone came out unscathed. But know this: every illustration takes on weight, so it must be able to pay its fare if it is to come on board. Answer honestly whether the details that interest you so much are crucial to the story's significance. A solid ability to trim, and a steely eyed willingness to toss an illustration off the ship, will let the right story shine.

---

11. Davis, *Wondrous Depth*, 29.

If you can wholeheartedly offer yourself to your listeners, good fruit will grow in that community. You will be shaping a healthy congregational culture, one in which it is okay to be limited and in process. You will model the reality that growth is a process, one marked by desperately needing and then stumbling upon grace, soaking it in like a plant takes in sunlight, and flourishing in its warm light. The beauty is that the practice of testimony will also bear lovely fruit within you. You will experience the freedom of being known and loved for who you are as you serve and lead your congregation. You will grow in the capacity to pay attention, to be poised on a lookout tower for the work of God in your life.

I have repeatedly felt the power of the intentional and careful use of the first-person-singular speech in sermons. Given how much testimonial speech resonates with our listeners, I am regularly surprised by how easily it slips off students' screens in my preaching classes. It is as if slashing through the exegetical and theological weeds consumed every ounce of their energy. The "aha" insight they finally found was so compelling that it seemed capable of standing alone if it was set forth logically and described eloquently. I will sometimes ask, "Where were *you* in this sermon?" and hear a sheepish, "Oh, yeah." If you find that "I" language is consistently missing in your preaching, here are four questions to ask yourself and four practices to try.

Ask This:

- How did my family-of-origin storytelling culture (or lack thereof) shape me in this area? Was it safe in my childhood home to laugh at ourselves? Did we admit our mistakes in stories around the dinner table, or was that met with scorn or indifference?
- What do I fear most about being known in my congregation?
- When I contemplate telling a vulnerable story, who are the specific listeners whose disapproval I most fear?
- In what ways does my worry about vulnerability diminish my capacity to lead?

Try This:

- End the next personal story you tell with a pivot to second-person singular, then another pivot to first-person plural, like this: "For *you*, this may play out in an entirely different way. Maybe you hit this struggle at work more than in your relationships. But *all of us* can relate to the struggle to ____."
- Set aside some time to pay careful attention to your life. Reflect on the events of each day in all their pain and delight. Find a partner or use a journal to practice the *Examen of Consciousness*, a simple Ignatian practice of reflecting thoughtfully on one's day. Links to resources for learning this practice are below.[12]
- Practice intentionally offering your life in daily conversation, letting your stories testify to God's provision, to your blundering attempts to follow Jesus, and to the small but beautiful glimpses of grace in the quotidian stuff of life.
- Practice connecting with the characters of Scripture. As you read a passage of Scripture, listen for its unstated emotional cadences. For example, the text of Luke 2 does not say how the shepherds, Mary, or Joseph felt, but what do you imagine each felt as the story unfolded? Then, list those emotions and survey your life for instances where you have experienced those emotions.

First-Person Plural: The Host

The aromas entice us the moment we enter. The laughter from the guests already in the room draws us in. The hosts greet us warmly. We are eager for the meal ahead but glad that it begins with a pause to thank the Creator of this sumptuous food. As we take our seats, we breathe a contented sigh, savoring the sheer grace it is to be brought to this space and given this time, set apart to connect and linger. It feels refreshing to be hosted well. You

---

12. Ignatius of Loyola developed the *Prayer of Examen*, a powerful way of reflecting on one's life in the presence of God. A book which describes the process well is *Sleeping with Bread*, Linn and Linn, and consider this article: https://www.ignatianspirituality.com/ignatian-prayer/the-examen.

have felt it as a guest, I hope, and you have probably offered it to others around your table.

When we preach, we are hosting—inviting friends and strangers to gather, welcoming them to the table, and nimbly guiding the conversation around it. We always come as a guest as well, grateful to be fed together by the unseen Host in our midst. But at this moment, we draw upon the skills and vocation of a gracious host. We set the table for shared feasting upon the word as we name the struggles, joys, and hopes we hold in common. Hosting calls for *we* and *us* language.

Personal testimony (first-person-singular speech) may prepare us to hear the truth, and some listeners will quickly identify with our stories, intuitively connecting them to their own lives. But not all will, so we need language that gets everybody on board. That is where the first-person plural comes in. The preacher is still right in the mix, but instead of testifying on their own behalf, they dare to articulate on behalf of the whole. As preaching professor Thomas Long puts it, you come from the congregation,[13] but you come with a leadership role; you influence us as you name and include us all. You are leading as a savvy host does.

We language sets the table of the sermon and invites us to take our seats for the meal ahead. If from the start, listeners feel that they are seen and known, they will assent to the harder work that also may need to happen around this table. The preacher-host beckons us to reckon honestly with an aspect of our human nature or societal injustice that has been laid bare by the word and to hear how God speaks into that messy reality. When he or she pellucidly articulates the problem, tendency, or need we all experience, we lean forward, hungry for the nourishing word that satisfies our hunger or is medicine for our diseases. So, in your exegetical work with Scripture, as you ferret out the foibles of people long ago, ask relentlessly how those tendencies are just as present in us today. Be on the lookout especially for these fundamental truths about humans, as they resonate with your Scripture text.

First, and of first importance for preachers to see clearly, we are beautiful. We are of infinite worth. The most curmudgeonly of us are capable of immense kindness and the seemingly shallow can offer surprising insights. We are lovable here and now, just as we are. You will not get far as a preacher if you do not genuinely like humans, specifically those God has called you

---

13. Long, *Witness of Preaching*, 101.

to love and lead. Cultivate affection for the people who grate on you, and never take for granted the people you ostensibly cherish most.

Second, we humans are surprisingly capable of change by God's grace. You will not succeed at compelling people to change if you do not come to them with a fundamentally hopeful stance about their capacity for transformation by God's grace.

Third, we are sinful and broken, blind to the ways and work of God right in front of our noses. We are frighteningly alienated from God and one another, and we seem intent on staying that way. We fear change and resist it. As a result, we harbor the capacity for genuinely troubling levels of cruelty, self-deception, and ingratitude. Sober regard for the human propensity toward sin, even in the most charming and generous members, will serve you well as you preach.

Fourth, every one of us is bursting with longings, even those who seem to have it all. Hope for what we lack marks our human condition from birth to death. Longing for eternity has been planted in our hearts, but we distort and short-circuit that longing every day. We hunger not only for what we individually do not have or cannot do but for the world to be better and for our church to be more vibrant. It scares us to admit how much we long for some things. Many of us have endured a seemingly endless season of longing. Longing is exhausting and doesn't always end well. Ideally, it makes us hopeful and humble people, people who pray. But it can frustrate and immobilize us and lead us astray. Unmet longings can be the birthplace of addictions of various kinds. We are vulnerable to taking destructive shortcuts to fulfill our longings. Naming longings well allows us to speak into those tendencies. It also connects us, as it strikes a deep, resonant chord between us and the characters in Scripture, who were marked by deep and varied hopes as well—for home, for greatness, for identity, and healing.

Fifth, some of us are profoundly anxious about the future. Life on this planet involves countless unknowns and risks, and we have never felt more aware of that than as we recover from a global pandemic. Dark scenarios still abound. What is coming next, and how will it affect me? Fear can drive us to idols or a mad dash for the safest path. Fear makes us vulnerable to false and empty promises, and our culture is more than happy to feed them to us.

Sixth, some of us are suffering far more than we let on. Do not be deceived by the smiling faces and cheery greetings. As Buechner remarks, "As much as it is our hope, it is our hopelessness that brings us to a church of a

Sunday, and any preacher who, whatever else he speaks, does not speak to that hopelessness might as well save his breath."[14] Some listeners are doing all right, just dusting themselves off from the routine hits of their workweek or smarting a bit from the insolence of their teens as they enter the worship space. But some barely made it in the door. They are mourning the fresh and deep wound of a beloved friend's death, or they saw again just this morning how far from intimacy their marriage has drifted. We name with compassion the presence of mental illness, addiction, and familial estrangement that lurks beneath the shiny surfaces.

Seventh, we bring a vantage point as a community of interpretation, that causes us to see some things clearly and be blind to other truths within any passage of Scripture. In fact, we have several vantage points within any congregation, some of which are competing. One of our less comfortable roles as hosts is naming what we do not share. As we host, our uncomfortable task may be to bring to congregational consciousness the reality that some in our midst struggle to pay the rent while others add state-of-the-art entertainment centers to their vacation homes. Some live as regular victims of racial injustice while others live in countries where their ethnicity grants them privilege.

In this meal we are hosting, the view is quite different from the head of the table than from its foot, and that will change how various guests hear Jesus' words or take in Moses' decrees. Our social location and other aspects of our context will always color our view of a text, highlighting some features and obscuring others. Our role as host is to welcome every learner and listener to the Scriptures while guiding the meal's presentation so it both delights and nourishes everyone present. Let's notice how Jehoshaphat gathered and hosted his people in a time of crisis.

While it is not a sermon, Jehoshaphat's prayer models effective use of *we* language, naming collective fears and hopes. Like a wise host, Jehoshaphat brings the shared concerns of his people into the presence of God. In 2 Chronicles 20, we read that when faced with a horde of enemies, he gathered the people not to give his battle strategy but to name their collective situation in prayer.

First, he narrated God's past faithfulness in history. Then he described the present dire situation to God. Finally, he closed with this striking confession: "We are powerless against this vast army that is attacking us. We do not know what to do, but our eyes are upon you" (2 Chr 20:12). His

---

14. Buechner, *Telling the Truth*, 55.

leadership is remarkable in its freedom to name with honestly the current and unavoidable reality, and his own uncertainty as to how to lead in that moment. However, if the scene in Chronicles had ended with Jehoshaphat's earnest and humble plea, the battlefield would have looked quite different the next day.

Jehoshaphat's words created a space for another voice. Jahaziel took the microphone and shifted into the second person, bringing the people a prophetic declaration of the future work of God on their behalf. Hope and courage saturated Jahaziel's speech: "Listen, King Jehoshaphat and all who live in Judah and Jerusalem! This is what the Lord says to you: 'Do not be afraid nor discouraged because of this vast army. For the battle is not yours, but God's'" (2 Chr 20:15). Jahaziel then offered clear, specific advice for how to enter the battle. As leaders, we cannot fail to move to direct address, as Jahaziel does well here. But the people of Judah were better able to hear from him because Jehoshaphat had first hosted them well, naming their fears and gathering them up into his humble and public prayer.

Can there be too much *we* language in a sermon? Yes. Listeners need it, but it is far from all they need. When it overtakes a sermon, it can freeze our focus inward, emptying it of declarative force. A sermon seeks first to see what is happening within and around us clearly and then direct our gaze to the faithfulness of Jesus Christ. Sermons dominated by *we* talk may allow a present crisis to engulf us.

What does it take to host well, and why do we sometimes fail to do so? It takes *courage* to speak out of the testimonial, first-person-singular voice. It takes *care* to speak out of the first-person plural. For our hosting efforts to have integrity, they must come as the fruit of attending well all week long to the suffering and the joy of our beloved fellow travelers. We cannot name what we do not see, and we cannot see clearly from a distance. But, when we wade into the mess, muddying our clothes with our people all week long, we emerge with a strong, clear, and kind voice.

Preachers also leave out *we* language when they forget the fundamental realities of how persuasion works with humans. When we have labored to build a solid exegetical foundation and a robust theological argument, we can convince ourselves that we are all the way there. We think, "Surely if they just get this into their heads, they will be all set." But, like a tender seed, truth only takes root in softened soil. As you review your sermons, if this element is consistently missing, here are some questions to ask and practices to try.

Ask This:

- What assumptions about how persuasion works do I make which cause me to skip this step? For example, do I assume that if listeners are convinced intellectually of truth, they will change?
- What would need to change about my pastoring practices all week long for me to name our realities with greater integrity, nuance, and care?

Try This:

- This week, endeavor to listen well to those who show up on Sunday and those who likely never will. Follow five people on Twitter whose views are vastly different from your own. When you can connect with people in real time, work hard to ask the questions that take a conversation deeper, revealing longings and fears, regrets, and happiness. Ask a new question tonight of those with whom you share daily bread.[15]
- Read deeply and widely, including authors from different ethnic and racial backgrounds than your own. Fiction pierces to the core of the human condition. We become hosts of a more expansive table as we watch fictional characters choose well or poorly and see the fruit born of those choices. Thoughtful essays reflecting on painful current events can also make us wiser hosts.
- As you bring "we" language into your sermons, remember to describe our faulty tendencies gracefully. Come as a fellow struggler, and never to shame or condemn.
- On a delivery note, if you preach from a manuscript, know that it is especially critical to abandon those notes in *we* moments. Let carefully crafted phrasing go in favor of presence and connection.

---

15. The Gottman Institute is an excellent source for thoughtful questions between spouses or friends. https://intentionalmarriages.net/mp-files/love-map-questions.pdf/?force_download=false.

2

Preacher as Shepherd

The Promise of Second-Person Speech

"Blessed are *you* when people revile *you* and persecute *you* and utter all kinds of evil against *you* falsely on my account. Rejoice and be glad, because great is *your* reward in heaven."

MATTHEW 5:11

WATCH HOW JESUS SHIFTS his sermon into high gear when he hits the final Beatitude in Matthew 5:11. Up to then, he was describing the blessedness of people whose lives and hearts are marked by meekness, mercy, and the impulse to make peace. He built agreement about a set of counterintuitive yet resonant truths with those general statements. But in verse eleven, the verb form shifts from the third to the second person. He makes a subtle yet significant shift from generic speech about concepts to a direct address to people in pain. He pitches the ball straight to them, moving from describing to blessing and promising. I imagine him leaning forward with urgent intensity. He has been looking thoughtfully out and around, but now he looks right at them. Direct address in speech functions like a flashing sign: "Bridge Out Ahead!" or, more happily, "Free Gourmet Dinner at Our Grand Opening!" Whether they are compelling readers to stop or to stop in, these signs shout, "Pay Attention! Don't Miss This!"

Jesus made the last promise of the Beatitudes—the incredible gift of a happy heart amidst suffering—to people who were currently smarting from the blows of brutal oppressors. They needed to hear this. Remarkably, he stays in the mode of direct address for most of the sermon, pouring out a torrent of warnings, commands, and promises all the way up to the final verses. As if to dial down the intensity as he concludes, he shifts back to more general (though by no means anemic) observations about what will happen to different listeners to his words. But for the bulk of his sermon, Jesus keeps his verbs in the second person.

This directness is part of why the crowds loved to listen to him. He was not content to speculate about how, theoretically, it would be better when giving a gift not to announce that loudly. Instead, he boldly warned them, "*Do not do that.*" Right next to his warnings, he warmly and confidently promised them God's care and provision. "Are you not of much more value than the birds of the air?" (Matt 6:26). Like a shepherd who walks among the sheep in the evening, touching and naming each one, Jesus touched the hearts of his listeners as he spoke these bold and yet immeasurably kind words.

Hundreds of years later, as the Reformers looked at a lackluster church whose preaching had become anemic, they were especially eager to renew the mode of *direct address*. They urged preachers to speak right to people with urgency and boldness. This conviction flowed from their sense of the lively nature of the word itself, in all its forms—incarnate, written, and preached. We can expect it to speak—regularly, intrusively, and straight to us if it is, in fact, alive. The author of Hebrews asserts, "The word of God is living and active, sharper than a two-edged sword" (Heb 5:12). This should alarm us and also excite us for what may happen when we gather to hear that word. Church historian Bard Thompson wrote,

> With the other great Reformers, Calvin shared the view that true preaching is God speaking. The preached Word was a veritable means of grace by which God elected to address his people and offer them his gifts of forgiveness, sonship, and a place within the family of faith. Therefore, true preaching held the inevitable possibility that the ancient words of Scripture and the human words of the minister might, by the action of the Holy Spirit, spring alive in the hearts of the hearers as the real, alive, effective Word of God.[1]

Today, direct address makes some of us squirm. It raises the intensity level of a sermon, which feels dicey. It may have gotten Stephen killed.[2]

---

1. Thompson, "Reformed Church in the Palatinate," 36–37.
2. No doubt it was the cumulative effect of his entire speech, but Stephen shifts

Some of us shift into it naturally, but others of us shy away, fretting about its downsides. It does come with some communicational land mines. Sermons entirely in direct address can feel too "hot," too intense. But we cannot fail to engage in it if we want our preaching to sound like—to resonate with—the speech events of the Bible or to catalyze transformation in the way that they did.

Often, we will find it more effective to work toward moments of direct address after first laying descriptive foundations through historical background, exploring and explaining the tricky aspects of a text. We build authority and trust as we walk with our listeners on that journey from confusion to clarity, from surface-level familiarity with a passage to deepened insight. As we noted, even Jesus did not begin the Sermon on the Mount in direct address. Instead, he drew his listeners close before speaking right to them. Similarly, if we move too quickly to direct address, we will lose some listeners, who are not ready to trust us to challenge them—or even to bless them. On the other hand, when we speak with insight about the Scriptures and with authenticity about our experience, we build confidence that we are trustworthy messengers who can send those truths deep into our listeners' hearts.

Sadly, some preachers never make the shift to direct address. Instead, they circle the shallow end of the pool, opining about generic truths, much like the teachers of the law in Jesus' day. They rarely offend listeners and rarely impact them, either. Direct address takes courage and confidence. It also takes love. It assumes an authoritative (not authoritarian) relationship with our listeners and it assumes that we care. We are invested. We are willing to risk and suffer. Direct address is a preacher's way of putting "skin in the game," and that skin can get badly scratched. We fear that our promises will meet with skepticism, our warnings will meet resistance, and our blessings will meet with indifference. They may. But when we decide to do it anyway, to look people in the eye and speak straight to their hearts, that is the very moment when preaching becomes clothed with power. Let's look at the primary ways speech in direct address wields that power: to promise, warn, and bless.

---

strikingly into direct address in his final, closing lines (Acts 9:51–53), and this did not help him win a friendly hearing.

We Preach in Direct Address to Promise

Promise is central to preaching's power. The wise homiletician Richard Lischer would go so far as to say that at its core, promising is the essence of preaching. He asks the pivotal question, "What kind of language flows from the speech act called the gospel?" His answer, unequivocally, is the language of promising. He writes,

> The promise is an ideal prototype for preaching. In terms of time and value, promise is first in God's order of speaking to his people (as Paul insists in Galatians 3:17), thereby indicating God's true preference for the kind of discourse he wishes to perpetuate with the church. The promise is not a quality in God-like love or an attitude in the believer like hope, but it is a genuine and familiar speech act whose nature has already been defined with linguistic precision. It lies close to the heart of the gospel, a relationship that is recognized in one of the original meanings of *praedicare*, "to promise." Most of all, it says and does what God intends for those he loves.[3]

A large part of what God intends for those he loves is that they believe in him and wholeheartedly trust in him. Luther grasped anew the mystery that when we hear God's promises, faith can arise in us in response. He wrote, "For God does not deal, nor has he ever dealt, with man otherwise than through a word of promise . . . We, in turn, cannot deal with God otherwise than through faith in the Word of his promise."[4] When we hear ourselves addressed with promises, we may of course respond with doubt or a hard heart, but Luther had high hopes that promise would catalyze new or renewed trust in God. He believed that the risen Christ roamed the aisles as preachers preached, kindling faith within their hearts in response to the gospel promises.

What makes promising risky? It inserts the promiser into the narrative. When I watch police or detective dramas, I always wince when the officer says to the grieving widow, "We *will* find the person who did this." I worry that they raise unrealistic expectations and set themselves up for a hard fall if they fail. But, heedless of those risks, they always promise that outcome. It may be a bit of bravado on their part, but I like what it does for them. They kick into gear. They bind themselves to use all their energy

---

3. Lischer, "Preaching and the Rhetoric of Promise," 71.
4. Luther, "Babylonian Captivity of the Church," 36:42.

to fulfill their vow. God does this when he makes covenants. God *enters* them, binding himself to do whatever it takes to keep and complete them. A promise brings the promiser right into the heart of the story. We cannot deliver promises from a distance.

Promises are inextricably tied to the character of the speaker. They only work when the recipient knows and trusts the one promising. When we hear a word of promise, if we are savvy, we do a little sleuthing to ferret out the reputation and intent of the one making it. If I am wasting away in a jail cell on false charges and a lawyer says, "I *will* get you out of here," that is only positive news if I trust that lawyer's integrity and capability. I will likely snoop around for testimonies about the law firm's track record. As my confidence grows, I allow myself to hope. I might even follow some of the directives they give me to strengthen my case.

As trust in the promiser grows, the promise engages and activates the recipient. As theologian Jürgen Moltmann writes, "The word of promise therefore always creates an interval of tension between the uttering and the redeeming of the promise. In so doing, it provides [people] with a peculiar area of freedom to obey or disobey, to be hopeful or resigned."[5] Moltmann adds the element of hope to the faith Luther understood promise fostered within us. Faith calls forth obedience, but hope sustains it. Abraham went out from Haran because he trusted in God's promises. They set him in motion. Hope kept him moving.

Who exactly is making the promises in a sermon? In this odd endeavor, we who preach dare to stand and make promises on God's behalf. Are we inviting them to trust God or us? Both. We promise as ones who have tasted and seen the reliability of God, so it is an act of testimony on our part. We jump in the pool, and from there, we can say, "The water is fine!" For promise language to be genuine, it must come from personal confidence in God. For it to be effective, it must come from a place of love for our listeners and freedom to express that. They will not trust us if they do not sense we are radically for them. When they risk assent to our bold words, we become a stepladder to faith in God, scaffolding on which they can stand as they learn to lean wholly on God. While scaffolding is temporary, the goal is not independence from preaching since new tests and challenges will always arise, and further embodiments of faith will need to emerge. New converts will need to hear the gospel afresh. The gathered

---

5. Moltmann, *Theology of Hope*, 104.

community's faith flourishes as it hears the word anew and interprets its promises for this moment.

When can promising go awry? While overpromising *always* works out in a crime show, many of us have heard harrowing stories of parents painting a castle in the air for their children, describing the dream house they will inhabit just as soon as the next deal comes through. We might have similarly heard of young disciples damaged because they believed expansive promises that they would be protected from all harm if they spent themselves in radical obedience. I once sat in heartbroken disbelief listening to a young couple returning from a cross-cultural mission where the promises had been outlandish, the pastoral supervision nonexistent, and the realities saturated with suffering. They said, "We are so *done* with all that. It is full steam ahead with our careers and goals from here on out." Overpromising does no one any favors.

Jesus makes many bold promises to his followers. Some are downright hard to believe, such as those about answered prayer. Some are hard to perceive. He promises that our lives will bear much fruit as we abide in him, and yet some of us do not see our lives overflowing with fruit. We await the visible fulfillment of that one. But he never promises that life will be free of suffering. In fact, he is clear that following him will lead to it. He promises the presence of the Holy Spirit to guide and sustain us. We who preach must be careful not to paint airbrushed pictures of endless and relentless happiness for our listeners if they only trust God. A brief word of warning here will suffice since the greater danger is failure to promise. So be wise but be bold, preachers—and I promise that God will be with you. Promising is ultimately one of the most joyful parts of our preaching vocation. Warning is harder.

We Preach in Direct Address to Warn

"I am *warning* you!!" This sentence, often delivered at an earsplittingly loud volume, is never one we want to hear. It usually caps off a heated dispute between, say, neighbors over the noise levels at last night's party. It comes with an unspoken threat: "Do this one more time, and the consequences will be dire." Few of us enjoy delivering or receiving a warning. But think about the last time you heard a hard but true word from someone you trusted. Your kindly doctor warned you that your cholesterol numbers were alarmingly high. A caring friend worried aloud that you seemed not just down, but downright depressed. You squirmed internally—it was not easy. But you listened well in those moments. They had your attention. You knew these people were not coming with these messages because it was fun for them, but because they wanted to see you flourish. That is precisely why we pastors engage in the hard work of warning.

A quick scan of communication events in Scripture, from the speeches of the prophets to the letters of the apostles, reveals that warning permeates their words. We must conclude that expressing it is something one does for people one loves. If we want our preaching to resonate with the spoken words of the prophets, apostles, and Jesus, we will need to be willing to enter the ministry of warning regularly. It is the work faithful shepherds do, with their bodies more than their words, as they steer the flock away from harm.

Sometimes, we warn because we can foresee harm that participants in some dangerous activity cannot. Unintended consequences to themselves and others can be more destructive than the consequences they do anticipate. The stakes are higher than they perceive. Sometimes, it is not so much foresight as insight we employ—as we notice a member engaging in practices in the realm of finance or the overuse of a substance and not making the connection with its harmful effects on their relationship with God and others. Insight is making those connections. Peter does that when he writes, "Be alert and sober *so you can pray*" (1 Pet 4:7). His readers may have known some of the benefits of sobriety but not linked it to their capacity to pray. Our role as wise leaders is to discern the interconnectedness of body, mind, and spirit in a world eager to detach these realms from each other.

We may also discern an urgency that others fail to see. They are closer to the cliff than they realize. We who are charged with the care of flocks must find ways to communicate urgency where complacency reigns. And we never warn in abstract generalities or vague descriptions. Warning calls for straight talk. In Scripture, the prophets were willing to warn boldly, and we can learn a lot from watching how they did it.

First, they often grabbed their listeners' attention with vivid imagery, depicting the harm in disturbingly graphic terms, whether Amos's basket of rotten fruit, Ezekiel's valley of desiccated bones, or Jesus' stark picture of a millstone tied around a person's neck. Why so explicit? To wake us up and shake us up. We are extraordinarily talented at lulling ourselves into complacency about our sin. We listeners use every tool we can reach to deflect blame, rationalize, and avoid looking it squarely in the face. Vivid imagery shocks us and restores our vision, forcing us to confront what we are avoiding. How might you bring vivid metaphors and analogies to your next sermon on sin and the harm it causes? What does the sin of envy smell or feel like? What color is greed? How does a recent news story exemplify our tendency toward pride?

Watch how writer Dorothy Littell Greco brings vivid imagery in her warning not to lose the opportunity in the pandemic for reflection on our latent idolatries. She describes a physical idol made of clay falling to pieces.

> That's why we need to pay attention in this season. When the idols topple, we can feel confused, angry, frustrated, agitated, and out of control. Those feelings can reveal where we have gone amiss. The pivotal moment that we find ourselves in can break the idol's spell. If we let it. Now that their fragility and impotence have been exposed, we all have a choice to make. Will we gather the pieces of the fallen idols and attempt to put them back together? Or will we recognize where we have been bowing down to idol gods, forsake them, and reorient ourselves back toward God?[6]

Vivid imagery drives the truth home, and Jesus did not shy away from warnings of houses falling in the sand or millstones tied around necks. As we look at how he and others engaged in this unenviable ministry, we also notice that they do not leave us gazing miserably at our sin. They compel us to take a close, hard look, but then they offer us compassion. They encourage us that change is possible, and ultimately call us to fix our eyes on Jesus. When we preach, we want to do the same. Therefore, warning will rarely be the heart of a sermon. When John the Baptist preached it was the appetizer, main course, and the not-so-tasty dessert. He had a specific vocation; but most of us are engaged in preaching as an extended conversation, so warning will be a side dish or even just the spice that enlivens the meal. We know how Jesus felt about disciples lacking in salt. So spice it up. Warn us away from dangerous paths because you love us, but do not leave us stranded there.

A warning is rarely the best note on which to end one's sermon. Granted, Jesus essentially did end his greatest sermon that way: "and it fell with a great crash" (Matt 7:27). So did Malachi, whose book ends on the cheery note, "lest I come and strike the land with a curse" (Mal 4:6). These

---

6. Greco, "Reflections: Idolatry," https://www.dorothygreco.com/reflections-on-covid-19-week-two-idolatry.

authors had their reasons for stark endings, but in general, even in letters with a strong dose of warning, Paul and other biblical writers end on the note of blessing. In the end, preaching is *good news*—so let us endeavor to make the gospel turn toward grace, mercy, a fresh start, the hope of transformation. Let us tell the great news that Christ has made a better path for us and we can choose to walk it. The writer of the book of Hebrews wrote many strong words of warning. He or she asks us to take a hard look at all that hinders our race, but in the end, the writer turns our gaze to Jesus, the pioneer and perfecter of our faith. The writer does not leave us in a puddle of shame and despair but spurs us on with the vision of Jesus, our guide and our journey's end.

As important as the ministry of warning is, its potential to go awry is perhaps even starker than that of promise. One reason is our natural tendency to scapegoat, which leads us to rail against external threats. When we find ourselves in the middle of a painful story, we search for a villain, and we line ourselves up as far as possible from that villain. You may have been in congregations where the harm or vice is all externalized, conveniently located in those people who vote the other way than we in this congregation do. If so, you know how that can rob preaching of grace and power. It allows listeners to avoid their complicity.

When we locate the harm within ourselves, we are off to a better start. But we can still easily slip into shaming and condemning words. One of the best antidotes to a shaming tone is vulnerable testimony. When we can speak as fellow travelers on the way, our listeners will hear that we are all on the same team. We look at our sins and struggles together, the way that caring doctor looks *with* us at our dismal cholesterol numbers and strategizes alongside us to bring them down. That doctor can warn while also articulating hope for renewed vitality. That is the work of blessing.

We Preach in Direct Address to Bless

Jacob must have known that Joseph needed an extra injection of strength to cross his life's final goal line and forgive his brothers for the wreckage they had caused. At the end of his days, Jacob is in the blessing business. He blesses most of his sons (a few get coal in their stockings), but his blessing for Joseph is over the top (Gen 49:22–26). Through eyes dim with age, Jacob looks intently at his son's life, wielding more perspective than Joseph could muster. He celebrates the fruitfulness of that life, depicting it as a lush vine running over a fence. He then names his son's pain—hostile archers shot at him hard—and describes how the Lord helped him to press through and overcome it. Finally, he heaps on him the blessings "of the heavens above and the deep below." It is my favorite blessing in Scripture. It flows from the heart of a father who aches over the suffering his son endured, yet who remains confident that God has been working for Joseph's flourishing—and his family's. I believe Jacob's blessing enabled Joseph to complete his life's final challenge. When we bless, we strengthen.

Blessings live in an odd space halfway between prayer and declaration. We do not hold the authority to grant what we bless people with, as God does when God blesses. And yet, as we stand in the tradition of Jacob and Paul, we humans are graciously authorized to voice those desires as more than simply desires. They are robust declarations and bold expressions of hopeful love spoken in the presence of the God who can bring them to pass. Blessing is liminal speech that prays to God even as it speaks to humans. Taylor captures the rich power in it when she writes,

> To pronounce a blessing is to participate in God's own initiative. To pronounce a blessing is to share God's own audacity. This may be why blessing prayers make some people uncomfortable. As a loyal member once said in my hearing, "I don't want to be that important." Yet she relied on me, her priest, to say the blessings she was unwilling to say herself—because she knew they were necessary, because she needed to hear a human voice pronouncing God's blessing on her the same way she needed food and water because otherwise, she might give in to the insistent idea that she truly was not important.[7]

Because we who are listening in church matter deeply to God and those who love us, we are worthy of blessing. Because we get beaten down by life, as Joseph was, we need it repeatedly and insistently pronounced upon us. Some of us who preach did not have parents who modeled this well, so it will not come naturally. Even for those of us who heard kind words daily as children, it will be a skill we need to sharpen, an intentional practice we'll need to pursue. That work will pay off as we lead others. Blessings take the promises of God and plant them into the hearts of those we lead. They make warnings hearable, for they assure our listeners that we admonish in love. When you preach, promise a lot, warn a power-packed little, and bless extravagantly.

7. Taylor, *An Altar in the World*, 206.

Ask This:

If you find that verbs in the second person for direct address are consistently missing from your sermons, ask yourself:

- What frightens me most about shifting into direct address?
- Have I ever heard a preacher, or a parent, warn others in a way that shamed or condemned? Has that contributed to a fear of warning in my preaching?
- Is it harder for me to promise, warn, or bless? Which one comes naturally to me? Why?

Try This:

- Look back over the last sermon you preached. Don't just think about it. Pull it up on your screen. Scan it for the lines of direct warning, promise, and blessing. Are you pleased with the level of direct address, or is it weak or altogether lacking? Where in the sermon could three more sentences of direct address have added potency? Now, say them aloud. What impact would that have added? How does it feel to say those lines?
- Think about the next sermon you will preach. You will probably best articulate the core truth in the third-person singular. ("Jesus replaces fear with faith.") From there, how will you take that truth and speak it straight to us, so that its implications for us land? Will that best be done with words of promise, warning, or blessing?

3

Preacher as Proclaimer

Declaring God's Goodness with Third-Person-Singular Verbs

> "If mercy were something God simply had, while his deepest nature was something different, there would be a limit on how much mercy he could dole out. But if he is essentially merciful, then for him to pour out mercy is for him to act in accord with who he is."
>
> —DALE ORTLUND

I SAT DOWN TO dinner feeling sheepish and nervous. I glanced from one unsuspecting parent to the other and then back down at my plate, mustering the courage to tell them what I had done that day. It was early spring of my senior year of high school, and I had made a rash offer to a classmate without thinking about how it would affect my family. Cindy was about to turn eighteen, so she was aging out of the foster care system and had nowhere to go. She was describing her plight as we stood by our lockers when I blurted out, "You can stay with us for a few months!" Then I gulped, instantly realizing that a better order of operations would have been to go home, ask my parents, and come back to Cindy with an offer the next day. As I shared this with my parents over dinner, I wondered just how much trouble I would be in for not asking their permission before glibly declaring that. I did not need to wait long; my father's reply was swift and decisive. "I am *so* happy that you did *just* what we would have done!" Then he simultaneously beamed, teared up, sighed like a man savoring his favorite meal, shook his head as if at the wonder of it all, and said again, "This makes me *so* happy!"

Looking at my dad, I felt a mix of amused bewilderment, palpable relief, and the dawning of an epiphany. I realized that deep down, I had not been afraid at all. I had intuited that my parents would be fine with my spontaneous offer. I realized that I had been in two schools all those years, learning biology and history at one, and how to be a human and a follower of Jesus in the other. I had watched what my parents did for stray cats, lonely international students at the holidays, or neighbors in distress on any day. That night my dad said, in effect, "You have seen what we tend to do, how we respond when we hear of someone in need. Today, you showed that you were paying attention." While it arguably would have been a great idea to check in with them first (and perhaps learn Cindy's history of violence before we experienced it firsthand), I have always been grateful for the grace shown to me at that moment. I still smile, remembering my dad's sheer pleasure upon seeing that someone who was watching how he lived and what he tended to do had caught his values.

We use the third-person-singular verb form to say what a person does (or did—we will meld past and present here). For example, imagine you are describing a friend who is a school principal to someone who has never met her. You might begin with physical attributes, but you will likely move to her habitual actions. "She greets each student by name as the school day begins." "She always makes time for parents with concerns." Each one forms a brushstroke as you narrate the characteristic things they say and do. Together, these patterned actions portray that person's essence. She acts and speaks this way because she is this way.

In this chapter, we will claim the third-person singular for one purpose only: to describe the activity of God, as that reveals the nature and character of God. Why only God here? After all, humans also do all sorts of fascinating things as they walk around the planet. They endlessly amuse, confound, disgust, and inspire, and that is a tale we need to tell. We have already discussed how to offer our own stories as witnesses and name the longings of our congregations as hosts, and we will continue to refine our telling of the human story in future chapters. Humans matter. But the sermon has a unique charge to render the biblical story's main character well. So here we will focus like a laser beam on how we talk about God—how we watch God at work the way I watched my parents, picking up traits and taking cues from their actions to the point where I could intuit their response to a new situation. Describing what we see and know about God is the dimension of preaching that we call *proclamation*.

Roles in Proclamation

The rather unfortunate English term for one who proclaims is a *herald*. It is the best translation for one of the most common Greek New Testament words for a preacher, a *kerux*. This term is regrettable mainly because we have no precise modern-day equivalent. The last time heralds were gainfully employed was about the 1700s, when they rode into European towns on horseback and shouted out proclamations the king or provincial ruler had made. That can strike us as a dated and unattractive picture of preaching. The town crier had little love for his listeners, no call for creativity or improvisation, and his job was done when he had read the proclamation, whether the listeners understood it or not. He mounted the horse and galloped on to the next town.

While the image of a herald has never gained much traction in my conception of preaching, there is no escaping that the related verb, to proclaim, is everywhere in the New Testament. John comes proclaiming God's strange and wonderful kingdom as Mark's Gospel opens, then Jesus takes over, and never stops. Paul becomes a bold proclaimer and calls those who engage in it to live out of boldness, close communion with God, and utmost fidelity as they retell the words they heard. The moment of proclamation is our summation of where the text has been going and how it reveals the story's Subject. We will not attempt to revive the word *herald*; instead, we will retrieve the best of the herald's role and speak of the preacher as a bold, sassy, and faithful proclaimer. It is striking how many sermons fail to turn the corner onto this street. Why, if it is so central, does that crucial moment of robust proclamation fail to transpire or be given adequate space to land with impact? I have three prime suspects.

First, those of us committed to rooting our sermons in one primary text may find that somewhere during the week, we got lost inside that text. Its peculiarities captivated and confused us, its strangeness and distance from our cultural moment troubled us, and its loveliness delighted us. Imperceptibly, the target for Sunday shifted and narrowed to resolving the questions of *this one text*, rendering *it* memorably and clearly. Wallace Alston articulates this tendency well. "The problem with many supposedly biblical sermons is that the preacher remains inside the text, as one might do when studying a Shakespearean play, wandering about the storyline . . . without reflecting on the role and place of the text within a coherent theological vision of reality."[1] We fail to do the summative work that shows how this specific text fits in the overarching story, as it declares the loveliness and power of our God.

A second reason for the failure to proclaim is our race to a text's relevance for us and our problems right now. If I had looked at my dad across the table that night and thought, "Well, thank goodness he wasn't angry at me," pouncing on the moment and its meaning for *me*, I would have missed the way that his words encapsulated and revealed my father's enduring character. This choice shrinks the focus to the implications of a text for *us*. We see this, for example, in the decision when preaching on the prodigal son to end the sermon with the predictable question, "Which son are you most like?" That approach rightly invites people to reflect on each young man's tendencies and consider their biases toward recklessness or resentment. It is a question eminently worth pondering, and it takes listeners right into the story. It is an excellent rest stop or scenic vista on the way to the destination. But it is not the story's *end*. We are not ultimately the subjects of that story, and neither was either son. Jesus renders a portrait of his Father by describing what one unbelievably merciful father did. If we fail to turn our listeners' gaze toward a sustained contemplation of the breathtakingly gracious Father depicted here, we have not fully preached this story's good news.

What else keeps us from arriving at that moment where we declare the beauty and goodness of God? The third reason is that it is not easy to do well. A few of the other modes of speech outlined in this book are less demanding and bring quicker payoff. That makes them more likely to dominate or even hijack the sermon. Some of them are more likely to feed our egos or meet listeners' expectations. For example, listeners crave practical advice for succeeding at work on Tuesday or relationally on Friday, which is not wrong in and of itself. (In our paradigm, this is the mode of third-person plural—wisdom for daily living.) But it can quickly crowd out proclamation. Numbers tend to grow when word gets out that a contemporary sage is dispensing tips that make life go better, especially when they come packaged in snappy sound bites we can retweet during the sermon.

---

1. Alston, "Recovery of Theological Preaching," 223.

Problem-solving preaching yields the quickest positive feedback. Unfortunately, when we hear that affirmation, we tend to lean into that mode, and we can inadvertently fail to root it in the source of all wisdom, the one without whom it is mere self-help drivel. I watched a preacher with much insight into human nature and a talent for describing it walk too far down this road, leaving the gospel behind. It became the less exciting story than the human drama, in his telling of it. The journey back was not an easy one. Who wants to watch listener acclaim recede like the waves at low tide? The choice to proclaim God's glory is intrinsically a choice away from more ego-gratifying forms of speech. While ultimately more life-giving and formative, listeners may not flock to hear it at the same rate.

What are the costs of the failure to proclaim God's beautiful ways? Thomas Long, describing preachers who stop short of proclamation, laments, "They speak affirming words, forgiving, and accepting words, words of prophetic challenge. But all these words are finally not enough. We must ultimately speak about God[,] . . . the things God is doing and saying because we want to shape our life according to the pattern of God's life."[2] Here, Long gives one excellent reason for speaking about God—its formative capacity. As we catch glimpses of how God works, we are inspired to imitate God's ways and live differently in response.

An even more vital outcome may be what transpires *between* listeners and God. When we render Christ well, those who see that portrayal will find themselves stepping back in awe even as they draw closer in renewed intimacy and trust. I got a glimpse of how this works when I was fighting a bad cold and weary from hours of standing in hot, crowded halls full of art in the Hermitage Museum in St. Petersburg, Russia. Then, I turned a corner and suddenly found myself right in front of Rembrandt's *Return of the Prodigal Son*. Stunned, I drew a deep breath and stilled my spirit to take it in. I felt those hands resting on my shoulders; I tasted that mercy. It pulled me in, magnetically and mysteriously. I wanted not only to behold this picture but to breathe it in and let it mark me. I found myself praying. It was an unforgettable moment of worship of the God revealed by that exquisite portrait.

If we believe with Luther that Christ "walks the aisles" when we preach, it should not be too much to hope for those moments to happen within our listeners during our sermons. We feel all too keenly that we are nowhere near the preaching equivalents of Rembrandt, but fortunately, our

---

2. Long, *Testimony*, 109, cited in Pasquarello, *We Speak*, 19.

confidence has never been in our ability. We do not preach to manufacture or engineer encounters with God for people—we are not that skilled, and that is not how it works, fortunately. We hope that our sermons can at least clear a space for them. One of the best things we can do throughout our preparation is regularly and boldly pray for those holy moments. Such encounters bring about even more than formation and imitation, but holy transformation.

Moments like that in sermons lead listeners (including the one preaching) into God's presence, where all sorts of surprises happen, including healing, the dropping away of a bitterness long held, a startling injection of fresh joy. We find our boarded-up hearts pried open; we find a new capacity to trust. We enter into worship, where we simultaneously stand back in awe at the bigger picture of God we have glimpsed and draw near, eager to be close to this majestic and merciful God. The capacity to describe God faithfully requires us to live into specific roles that we who preach may initially resist and to practice strange habits. Let me challenge you to embrace three identities, then point us to some practices we can pursue as proclaimers and describers of God.

Theologian

Most pastors shy away from describing themselves as theologians. They worry that it is a presumptuous overreach to label themselves in that lofty way. And the sad truth is that many pastors do not spend time cultivating theological depth, so it would be an overreach. We acknowledge most pastors are not as highly trained as those who are professors of theology. Here I intend a humbler and broader meaning of the word, which points to a calling every pastor should embrace. William Alston and Cynthia Jarvis urge pastors to assume that role. They write, "A striking fact about the church in our time is that where ministers pursue their calling as ecclesial theologians the church lives . . . and where they do not, the church tends to be trivialized and languishes."[3] In urging us to be ecclesial theologians they are calling us to let the contexts and questions of our faith communities drive our theological inquiry, so that the doctrines we proclaim are targeted medicine for what afflicts us today.

In this broader understanding, a theologian is simply one who takes care to know God well, who views life through the light of Jesus Christ. A

---

3. Alston and Jarvis, eds., *Power to Comprehend with All the Saints*, xiv.

theologian reflects upon the world and their circumstances through the lens of the promises of God. Robert Smith Jr. sharpens the point by inviting pastors to view themselves as *contemplative* theologians. To contemplate is to look at one thing for a sustained period, giving it one's attention and intention. Smith writes, "What is contemplative theology? It is being available to God, brooding over God, hovering over God and God's word, delighting in God."[4]

It is hard to brood and hover over One who seems to be constantly in motion. If we were in a studio attempting to draw a portrait of God, our cry would be, "Could you *please* sit still for a moment!" God is ever on the move in the narrative of Scripture and the life of the church in the world; it is we who must be still, take it all in through contemplation, and over time come to know God. The Lord invites us to be watchers in chief, finding the patterns in his habitual actions. To do that, we must stand back enough to glimpse the whole board, straining our arms wide to hold the tensions within the canon of Scripture and the doctrines of our faith. And we must come near, like the photographer who thrills to capture the intricate lines of grasshopper's wings in the sunlight. I watched my dad over many years and then looked in wide-eyed wonder during that moment around our table that disclosed his values so completely.

Similarly, as contemplative theologians we read and learn the story daily, and then we zoom in to notice the contours as Jesus stops to hear in full the pain of the woman with the flow of blood. We wonder at the grace of the Lord as he names, honors, and elevates a woman who had been at society's furthest margins. We hover over this story until we can reverently proclaim the character of the one who acts in these startling ways.

Theologians pay attention to Scripture and life, linger long enough to notice, and delight in what they see. Then, we who preach go a step further, pressing that into proclamation for the sake of our church's flourishing. Augustine wistfully acknowledged his desire to stop at delight when he admitted, "Nothing can be better, nothing sweeter than to gaze upon the Divine treasure without noise and hustle. To have to preach, to inveigh, to admonish, to edify, to feel responsible for every one of you—this is a great burden, a heavy weight, a hard labor."[5] Fortunately, he rose to the challenge and brought the fruit of his deep theological contemplation to the church.

---

4. Smith, "Preaching as a Contemplative Task," 164.
5. Augustine, cited in Brown, *Augustine of Hippo*, 253.

Moreover, he embraced the calling to be a teacher of the church—another identity we may resist.

Teacher of the Church

Those who complete an MDiv sometimes find themselves making self-deprecating jokes around their degree's title, especially when narrating its full name at a secular college reunion. "Why yes, I *have* mastered the divine." Today, it is an awkward title, but its original meaning implied a humble and faithful vocation. The word *master* comes from *magister*, Latin for a *skilled practitioner who teaches others*. Unlike teachers in schools who watch students complete a degree and move on to focus on the next batch of students, our work as teachers of the church is never finished. In faith communities, school is always in session. That is partly because our congregations are hopefully growing numerically, and newcomers need catechesis, training in the basics of the faith. But even with longtime disciples, we listeners are disturbingly forgetful creatures. And we keep getting into trouble or stumbling into new settings where the old formulations no longer fit. We need to hear timeless truth articulated in fresh, timely ways that resonate with the unique struggles and opportunities we face as individuals, churches, and members of our communities.

Worship Leader

We usually think of the worship leader as the person holding the guitar or seated at the piano. I urge preachers to see themselves as members of the worship team, whether or not they possess musical talent. They are part of the team that is wooing the congregation into God's presence. Another unfortunate aspect of the herald image is that historically heralds were tasked with dispatching the news in a neutral, dispassionate tone. Plenty loud, to be sure, but not expressing their joy or sorrow regarding the information they shouted. But we are different. We know and love the king we proclaim, and we want our listeners to love him more. Our study of God has led us to an even greater love for God.

Smith writes, "Contemplative theology is the cradle of doxology. It exists to praise God. . . . Something ought to be summoned within us, evoked in us, when we think of God."[6] We lead people into worship in these moments of proclamation, inviting them to come near to find healing for their estrangement from God. The blows of the week have built up defenses against fully trusting in God. We chip those away as we declare, "Jesus Christ has shown us the face of a God who turns toward us in love. God is entirely worthy of all your trust." We need to be careful theologians, faithful teachers, and joyful worship leaders to do that. Once we have embraced those roles, what practices can we pursue to proclaim God's beauty and truth well?

Practices

Here I offer you a set of practices that will help you proclaim God's character with freshness and fidelity. The first two are preparatory, helping you ferret out the good news each doctrine carries and explore it from multiple angles. The third is an encouragement to be intentional about the moment of proclamation in your sermon.

First Practice: Find the News in Scripture's Truths— and Show How It Is Good

When the people of Israel went into exile, every paradigm that told them how God worked was shattered. What did it mean that God dwelled in their midst when their temple was no longer anywhere near them? The prophets proclaimed familiar truths retooled and reframed for that challenging season. Those well-known truths came to the Hebrew people as news, hard to grasp and yet freshly relevant in their new setting. As we emerge from a global disruption that has shattered many of our settled paradigms, we who lead have a unique opportunity to do the same. Our challenge is not finding brand new news—that is usually called heresy. Our challenge is to discern where familiar truths have been forgotten, eclipsed, or engulfed by current circumstances. What good news has become difficult to believe? What timeless truth needs to be articulated and lived out afresh now?

N. T. Wright explores this in his book *Simply Good News: Why the Gospel Is News and What Makes It Good*. He offers the analogy of a couple hearing the news that their beloved and desperately ill child will recover.

---

6. Smith, "Preaching as a Contemplative Task," 160.

Tests are showing that the latest treatment is working! From there, Wright makes several striking points about the nature of good news. First, it always comes to us as an unexpected development within a longer story, a larger context. In this case, the story starts with the news that their child is gravely ill. Secondly, although positive news announces a past event (the lab results came back with encouraging data), it alters the present and the future. As Wright notes, "[T]his news is about something that has happened, because of which everything will now be different. This news has significance . . . it has consequences that alter lives."[7]

His most intriguing point is that news is rarely a done deal, ending the story. Instead, he insists, "[T]he news introduces an *intermediate period of waiting*. The child is still in the hospital—but instead of waiting anxiously and sorrowfully, we are now waiting with excitement and joy for her to get better and come home."[8] What disciplines will we need in the season of waiting? We invite people to cultivate patience, curiosity, and hopefulness. What will it look like for us to proclaim the work of God so that it lands like news that changes everything, and at the same time equips listeners to persevere while it seems that nothing is changing? Sometimes, that means confidently announcing events yet to happen, preaching the coming full redemption of our bodies and planet. Sometimes that involves careful listening to the current moment so that the news meets the need. Our work as tellers of good news is like that of a jeweler expertly placing an old diamond in a new setting, allowing its beauty to sparkle anew. As the great preacher P. T. Forsyth put it,

> The church is built up by . . . the repetition of its own old gospel. . . . The preacher is not to be original in the sense of being new but fresh. He is not the light; he but bears witness to it . . . But God forbid that I should (seem to) say a word to justify the dullness that infects the pulpit. But the cure for pulpit dullness is not brilliancy. It is *reality*. It is the directness and spontaneity of the common life. The preacher is not there to astonish people with the unheard-of; he is there to revive in them what they have long heard. He discovers a mine on the estate. The church, by the preacher's aid, must realize its own faith and take home anew its own gospel. That which was from the beginning we declare unto you—that fresh old human nature and that fresh old grace of God.[9]

7. Wright, *Simply Good News*, 3.
8. Wright, *Simply Good News*, 3.
9. Forsyth, "One Great Preacher," 416.

Second Practice: Gaze at the Gem from Many Angles

In your study of a passage, a core truth of our faith will usually begin to crystallize from that study. You will want to lift that out and set it apart for a closer look. Once you have identified that, what do you do next? How will you articulate it in a way that forms faith in your listeners? What could you do to add texture and depth to your proclamation of it? Here is what I recommend: isolate ninety minutes of concentrated focus on your doctrine, the core truth you will proclaim. More would be better, but I want you to do it. If you assume this task takes ten hours, you likely will not embark on it. With disciplined focus and a plan, one can accomplish a lot in ninety minutes.

Theological Warm-Up Exercise:

First, briefly review the articulation of this doctrine in the church's historical development. Books like Justo Gonzalez's *Essential Theological Terms*[10] and Alister McGrath's *Christian Theology Reader*[11] should be on your shelf or digitally accessible to help you do that.

Next, write one-sentence answers to these five questions:

1. How would our faith be *deficient* without this doctrine? What would be missing?

2. How is this doctrine *unique* to our faith—how does it set us apart from other world religions and secular belief systems?

3. How might listeners hear this good news as bad news? What do we need to be sure to say (and not say) to make sure that does not happen?

4. How is this truth radically refreshing news, for all time and for us in this specific time? For what toxins within us is it a healing tonic?

5. What image, metaphor, or story could bring this truth home to my listeners' hearts, helping them understand it, remember it, and savor its goodness?

---

10. Gonzalez, *Essential Theological Terms*.
11. McGrath, *Christian Theology Reader*.

Homiletical Warm-Up Exercise:

First, write one crisp sentence of testimony expressing why you are grateful for and newly astonished by this truth. This articulation will prepare you to expand that sentence in your sermon.

Now, complete these five sentences:

1. Because this is true, we no longer need to _____.
2. Because this is true, we are free to _____.
3. What this truth means for us when fears consume us at two in the morning is _____.
4. If our city or nation really grasped this, it would change _____.
5. What this truth might look like this coming Wednesday at school or work or around our tables at home is _____.

Third Practice: Find and Seize the Moment

The above exercise prepares you to proclaim a core truth of our faith well. But we can still let the pitch go by if we aren't on the lookout for where that best happens in each sermon. There is no one answer to that. As we get better at preaching, our eyes will be trained to discern the most effective moment for a summative and strong proclamation, and we will know how to seize it boldly. Sometimes it will feel like a summative conclusion, flowing inevitably from what has come before. Sometimes it will crash in like an intrusion, unexpected and therefore even more arresting and memorable because of that.

Effective preachers are willing to linger in that moment of proclamation, even to the point of discomfort or of sounding repetitive, as they restate a truth in a few different ways. As they do that, they are beckoning the truth to come home to listeners' hearts, looking for the opening in the walls we've built against it. It would be easier for one and all to move on quickly, to let the truth graze us rather than pierce us. But piercing is what the truth wants to do (Heb 4:12), and we can trust that ultimately it does so to heal. Our role is to trust that process and make space for truth to do its work. So slow down, look right at us, and let the moment of proclamation be a sustained and holy one.

We have discussed in this chapter the roles we must embrace as theologians who teach and lead others to glad and humble worship. We seek to contemplate God, as the consistent actions of the triune God reveal God's character. The practices described above will help you bring texture and depth to your proclamation, grounding it in the tradition of the church and extending it to the needs of today.

Ask This:

- The chapter identified three roles we must embrace as we seek to proclaim God's actions and character: theologian, teacher, and worship leader. Which of these comes most naturally to you? Which do you most need to cultivate?
- Look back on your last three sermons. How well did you do at proclaiming an aspect of God's nature? Were you able to find a way to state it that let it land with impact? Did you testify to your gratitude for this truth? Did you use some of the tools described here to teach it well? What would you like to do better?

Try This:

- The next time you state a striking truth about God in a talk or sermon, linger there. Let the impact of it land. Look into the eyes of those in the room (or into the camera sending this word to people you love). Long pauses often feel awkward, so you'll be tempted to speed past them, but they are gifts to your listeners. They create a space where they can hear God speak.
- If creativity in crafting a metaphor or analogy that communicates a truth about God is challenging for you, workshop that with a friend who is better at it or read authors who do it well. If precision and clarity in articulating doctrine is your growth edge, take time to write one clear paragraph explaining the doctrine in your next sermon well, drawing on the wisdom of the church and using the sentence completion exercises above.

4

Preacher as Sage

Teaching Wisdom with Third-Person-Plural Verbs

> "The one thing every Jesus follower needs every day is always the same: wisdom. In other words, we need an understanding of God's vision in action that will make a kingdom difference in people's lives."
>
> —MARK LABBERTON

WHEN YOU HEAR THE word *sage*, you may picture a pungent but scraggly gray-green bush. Or perhaps a wizened, bearded man pops into your mind. That's a little closer to my meaning here, but only a few of us readily identify with that picture. It is hard enough to relate to the image of a herald, but at least they got to tear into town on horseback and shout with all their might. Once we see the idea played out in the pages of the New Testament, it is downright exhilarating to step into the humble yet extraordinary role of a proclaimer of fantastic news. But a sage can seem even more remote from our sense of vocational identity. At worst, we imagine a guru in a distant tower dispensing enigmatic proverbs that barely relate to our lived experience. At best, we picture a kind and wise person offering insights that light up a new path we can walk. But even then, some of us struggle to imagine that wisdom coming from *our* mouths. Especially if you are on the younger side or newer to ministry, it may seem presumptuous to aspire to the role of sage. The word *sage* may never feel like a fit for you, just as I admitted in the last chapter that I've never warmed to the concept of a herald. Either way, my challenge to you in this chapter is to embrace the calling to preach deep and practical wisdom, in part by growing wiser yourself.

You need to preach wisdom because your listeners need it. They need to hear good news declared about God, and then they need that truth fleshed out so it can shape and equip them to live as faithful disciples in a world bent toward very different pursuits. To resist and transcend that pull, they will need a solid and clear understanding of how sin worms its way into our hearts and minds, how it persists on systemic levels, and the best soil in which the lovely fruit of the Holy Spirit grows. That is where the third-person plural comes in. It excels at describing how human hearts are formed and how life works ethically, spiritually, and psychologically—how the virtues God gives will lead to our flourishing and how vices and idolatrous practices will flat out wreck us. This chapter will ask whether our sermons equip listeners to take their truths home, pursue human flourishing, and skip the shortcuts that distract or spiral into destruction.

Technically, of course, many statements about "how life works" could be stated in the third-person singular. For example, "Love is patient; love is kind." Associating the third-person plural with preaching wisdom is admittedly one of our paradigm's less tightly fitting pieces. I hope you can use a phrase like *these paths lead to life* to help you remember that the third-person plural is the place where we assess our sermon's capacity to impart wisdom. We call people to walk the paths that lead to life as a natural outcome of our articulation of the nature of God—invitations to the ways of wisdom extend, flesh out, and deepen those proclamations.

Wisdom is not like a leakproof water bottle we purchase once and keep in our backpacks. Instead, it is the water itself that needs regularly refilling from clear streams. A sermon can be one of the best of those streams, and your listeners come thirsty every week. Some listeners might be content with (or even eager for) a consumerist arrangement where the church serves as a water filling station or drive-up window, a reliable and convenient but remote wisdom dispenser. The pandemic may even have fostered that mentality. But we want more for our life together and more for the dynamic between our congregations and us.

Our goal is not to dispense wisdom on demand, topping off their bottles with just enough for the week ahead. Instead, we preach to catalyze the formation of wise people who walk in wisdom and seek it together from its source. We want to see God form individuals and communities capable of savvy responses to troubling events, tangled family dynamics, and dry spells or dark places within their hearts. Our sermons model pathways for growing in wisdom, and they take listeners on shared journeys of discernment when the world feels confusing.

Preaching wisdom yields another surprising benefit. It unifies congregations. When we struggle with widely varying interpretations of current events, biblical wisdom grounds us in the core truths and values we share. Wisdom in those moments is the welcome equivalent of a deep breath. It invites us to step back from the chaos in our headlines and reflect together on their meaning, attempting to place them within Scripture's story. When emotions are running hot, sage insight and thoughtful perspective can calm and unite listeners as it gives voice to our common ground, the core values we all treasure, and the vulnerabilities we all share. Faithful preaching in these moments points out the sinful tendencies, idolatries, and temptations on *both* sides of an issue. Wise preaching is eminently hopeful, able to find the cracks where light may slip through even a profoundly painful moment—where the Holy Spirit may be doing unseen work. Something extraordinary might happen even within congregations whose arms have been cat-scratched by division when they hear words that resonate with core truths. They may even find that they can pray as one body and link arms to serve together.

Preaching wisdom benefits us enormously, but some of us still wonder if we are capable of it, especially if we are less seasoned in life. I am confident that you can preach wisdom, even early in your ministry, in part because you are not the source of that wisdom. The Spirit who speaks through Scripture is the source of knowledge and understanding. As you bring those words into conversation with your life, the life of the world, and the current struggles of the people you love, God will grace your words with wisdom. The psalmist was not (entirely) boasting when he said, "I am wiser than all my teachers, for I meditate on your law" (Ps 119:97). Scripture often names old age as one predictor and enabler of wisdom, simply because knowledge comes from reflection on experiences, and the old have more of those. Wisdom is making connections and seeing patterns—a skill that tends to grow with time and by having more dots to connect. But it does not always happen.

Wisdom is the capacity to look at past successes and failures in similar circumstances and discern a faithful path forward. It equips us to interpret and explain the varied events of the past for today. But time and advanced age is no guarantee. Many grow old with little capacity for self-reflection, or they draw the wrong lessons from events. Conversely, youth does not disqualify a person from displaying wisdom. Solomon, at a young age, asked God for and received wisdom. (If only it had lasted.) Jesus delighted the elders in the temple with his wisdom while still a boy. Likewise, young preachers can teach wise truths with great power if they are careful students of Scripture, their own life, and the lives of others, and if they have apprenticed and attached themselves to Jesus.

Though Scripture repeatedly urges us to seek wisdom, it is ultimately a gift. God gives it to those who ask for it, as we see from early in Solomon's life. Likewise, James encourages folks who lack wisdom to ask God, who gives it generously (Jas 1:5). But it is not a gift handed out indiscriminately, like someone on a busy street handing out flyers for a store's grand opening. Instead, it has an elusive and mysterious quality. It comes to us as gift but at the end of a diligent and dedicated search. Proverbs 2:1–10 portrays a person begging for wisdom, crying aloud for it, searching for it as for hidden treasure, and diligently applying his heart to understanding. But then Proverbs 8:1 flips the metaphor and depicts wisdom as a woman crying out in her eagerness to give wisdom to all who will receive it.

We hit one other wall as we consider whether we aspire to be a sage. Let's be honest: sages can be annoying. They can come off as self-righteous and out of touch, and their tone can be scolding. Further, they do not always know when to quit. Jesus had the discernment and discipline to stop dispensing his pearls, even when he had more in his pouch when he knew the timing was not right (John 16:12). But, unlike Jesus, we often back up our dump trucks, laden with our brilliant insights, and hit the release button onto our congregations. Those who pray for wisdom must also pray for even more enormous truckloads of restraint, humility, grace, and integrity—for insight about their insights. Finally, they must actively show their care in myriad small ways so that love is evident even as they speak hard truths.

As we seek to grow in wisdom, we learn from Scripture, of course, but an overlooked source is the wisdom of the church over the centuries. One of the specific ways sage saints sought to grow in knowing and living out wisdom was to put Scripture in a conversation with the ancient philosophers who pondered what they called virtues and vices. J. K. A. Smith distinguishes virtues from principles, writing, "Laws, rules, and commands specify and articulate the good; they *in*form me about what I ought to do. But virtue is different: virtue isn't acquired intellectually but affectively . . .

Education in virtue is a kind of *form*ation, a retraining of our dispositions."[1] We will explore how that formation happens and then consider how to communicate wisdom with freshness and impact.

Becoming Wise: Virtues and Vices

The very words *virtue* and *vice* seem stuffy and remote to us today, but they were downright exhilarating to the ancient Greeks and Romans. They understood that they attained virtues (and avoided or shed vices) through heroic contests with wild beasts, capricious gods, and impossible challenge courses, not unlike a competitive reality TV show today. Think Jason and the Argonauts slaying bulls and tricking dragons. That understanding led to competitions such as the Olympic games, which built into them virtues like justice, prudence, temperance, and fortitude. Philosophers widely agreed on these four virtues; various lists added a few more. These archaic terms can trip us up at the starting line, as a word like *prudence* may conjure images of a self-righteous prude. But its original meaning was rich and attractive—sea captains who possessed prudence could assess when to send a ship out on the sea and when to wait in the harbor. Prudence encompassed not only a call to safety but to courage—if conditions were right, the prudent captain did not hold back.

Augustine and Aquinas called the quartet of justice, prudence, temperance, and fortitude the natural virtues, which formed a foundation for the theological virtues of faith, hope, and love. These are infused by divine grace and not strenuous human effort. The abbess and extraordinary preacher Hildegard of Bingen contributed a lively play in which the vices and virtues vie for the affection of a disciple.[2] Both ancient and medieval saints found them to be trustworthy companions on their journeys to holiness. Preaching professor Michael Pasquarello explains, "As capacities for acting freely and for excellence, the virtues restore Christ's beauty to the human soul, awakening the intellect to know the truth and moving the will to love what is known."[3]

The idea of gaining virtues through strenuous effort in fierce competitions can seem wildly at odds with the biblical descriptions of the fruit that the Spirit freely lavishes upon us as gifts. God gives that fruit to build up

---

1. Smith, *You Are What You Love*, 18.
2. von Bingen, "Ordo Virtutum," in Dronke, ed., *Nine Medieval Latin Plays*, 147–84.
3. Pasquarello, *We Speak*, 131.

(not compete against other members of) the body of Christ. But, acknowledging the points of divergence, the saints persisted as students of wise secular philosophers. They believed that the best of their insights about virtues could teach them how to pursue Christlikeness, so they gleaned all they could. For example, the first insight the ancient Greeks grasped was that the virtues could *grow*—they were not static entities but rather were like saplings, which thrive when given sustained attention. In the case of virtues, they grew through disciplined practice. In the case of fruit, we understand that it is God who brings the growth, but we position ourselves for that growth to happen within us. We will explore the dynamics of transformation in chapter 9. For now, a firm conviction that deep and beautiful changes toward holiness are occurring within our listeners will make us hopeful as we preach, and an understanding that the process can be slow and messy will make us patient as we lead.

The second truth the ancients understood was that virtues grew best in *communities* where others shared their value. So, they created gymnasiums, live-in academies where promising youth who sought excellence could be tested and developed, not unlike Jesus' band of disciples. Surrounding ourselves with people who love what is good even more than we do is a great way to strengthen our devotion to it. Watching how they live fortifies us to practice habits that lead to flourishing.

Medieval theologians spent arguably more energy understanding the vices, in their quest to understand the contours of evil well enough to be armed against it. They identified one set (lust, gluttony, greed, wrath, sloth, envy, and pride) as particularly deadly because they saw them as *originating* sins, which generated others. For example, sloth gives birth to cowardice and despair. While this list focuses on personal temptations and sins, others rightly reflect on sin's corporate and systemic dimensions, as individual sins breed unjust policies, laws, and collective apathy.

My goal is not to pick apart the various secular and theological lists but to highlight that the church has understood for centuries that we grow wise by cultivating our love for what is life-giving and our repulsion from what is death-dealing. As we see how Christ is the source of all that makes us whole, our delight in and devotion to him grows. Pasquarello reflects on that ultimate end of the pursuit of virtue. He writes, "The virtues function to energize, integrate, and direct our capacities so that everything about us is disposed to a final end of happiness in friendship with God."[4] As we

---

4. Pasquarello, *We Speak*, 109.

preach toward that end, it will benefit us to contemplate them by reading the wise saints of today and long ago and teasing out aspects of a virtue or vice, a tendency, or a trait. That will give our sermons depth and texture. When we move from that deep background work to this Sunday's sermon, we may still find ourselves asking, "How can I teach and proclaim wisdom so that it feels fresh and attainable?"

Preaching Wisdom: Ten Stepping Stones

We all get stuck from time to time, whether in a relational rut or a pernicious habit. For preachers, that paralysis takes the form of a confounding inability to articulate what matters most about an idea. We feel stymied, like the moment on your hike when you come to a knee-deep and not so peaceful stream. The side you are standing on represents your solid, faithful exegetical work, which had yielded a clear truth you are passionate to bring to your listeners. On the other side is that truth expressed in language that is clear, crisp, and fleshed out for the week ahead. But how on earth do you get there? Scanning downstream twenty feet, you notice a set of sturdy stepping stones that can get you to the other side. Let me offer you ten stepping stones to a profound and fresh articulation of wisdom. Here we will assume that you seek to teach to illuminate the goodness of a virtue or the evils of a vice. Plant your feet on a few of these stones and see if they help you get across the stream.

1. Define It

While quoting a word's dictionary definition usually adds little real insight, a vivid and specific definition can spark a fresh perception. It makes the familiar strange, which engages the mind. As preachers, it can feel daunting to venture a new meaning for a concept. We wonder, "What qualifies me to add to the consensus on what *love* means?" Let me clarify that I am not asking you to craft a better *dictionary* definition that encompasses every aspect of a word's meaning for all time. Instead, I invite you to name the specific, timely, and perhaps startling sense that has emerged from your meditation on text and life for this sermon and boil that down to one tight phrase. When it comes to exposing our darker tendencies, a stark definition works like a light turned on in a dim cabin where we are settled in for the winter and have let the trash overflow. The preacher who is savvy about the vagaries of the human heart knows how to shine that light in ways that pierce and expose; they get us up on our feet to find the exit door to that grim place. Put more positively, when a preacher offers a fresh and beautiful description of hope or love, we listeners are drawn to it by delight and desire. Let's look at an example of each—defining to expose and defining to delight.

First, watch how preacher William White brings insight to sloth by his definition of it in a sermon. He begins by debunking a commonly held and inadequate description, which clears the ground for his sharpened one.

> People often confuse sloth with idleness. Some of the busiest people in the world are the most apathetic to those in need. Perhaps it is their very activity that causes them to be blind to the hurts of both the people closest to them and to the world's wounded. . . . Sloth is the sin of disconnecting ourselves from the rest of creation, from the rest of the human family.[5]

Did he redefine the word for all time? No. Disconnection is not the sum of sloth, which also involves laziness, despair, and apathy. But this definition lifts out and highlights one overlooked dimension. Disconnection becomes a portal into a fresh consideration of sloth. It might even cause me to ask where I am disconnected from creation and fellow creatures.

Watch how definitions of virtues can also draw us in. African American preacher and composer Charles Tindley (1851–1933) crafted a rich and beautiful depiction of love, rooted in the simple desire to make the beloved happy. He preached,

> Love is the soul of one person going out, with all its possession and powers, to make another happy. It is this going out to make others happy that is healing the scars and wiping up the blood caused by Cain's murderous club, and Samaritan-like, healing the wounded, providing for their comfort, and paying the bill. It is the sunlight of heaven caught and stored up in the human life to shine among men. Like chunks of coal, a heart full of the Love of God has banked the fires that are destined to burn up and melt the coldness of this world into the springtime of heaven.[6]

Theologian Josef Pieper puts forth *beholding* as an essential component of love. He defines love as the impulse and capacity to say, upon seeing

---

5. White, *Fatal Attractions*, https://www-ministrymatters-com.fuller.idm.oclc.org/library/#/bibthserm/8d4601ffafd3393fd44b1c21a6912f89/sloth.html.

6. Tindley, cited in Edwards, *History of Preaching*, 538.

another person, "It is good that you exist! How good it is that you are in this world!"[7] Of course, that does not cover the waterfront of our need to serve, trust, and forgive those we love, but it jolts us out of complacency as it invites us to behold the person before us with fresh wonder, gratitude, and delight. If crafting new definitions sounds like jumping to the moon, remember that it is perfectly acceptable to borrow them, as long as you give credit where it is due. So be on the hunt for them. Avidly read authors who excel at it, like C. S. Lewis, Dallas Willard, Kathleen Norris,[8] and Frederick Buechner.[9]

2. Name a Paradox or Tension

A paradox is an espresso shot to the brain. It jolts a groggy mind into active thought. We listeners strain to reconcile two seemingly contradictory statements that the speaker has had the nerve to claim are both true. The process of understanding how both claims can be valid is demanding, energizing, and satisfying. This makes a paradox a bolder gambit than a definition, one that may yield even more profound insight. Naming a paradox within a virtue or a vice allows us to articulate it with nuance and texture. That resonates. When preachers describe the tensions that make an excellent gift like hope complicated, we listeners breathe a sigh of relief. We say inwardly, "I always thought it was more complex than the wall hanging in the kitchen made it seem." When you as a communicator acknowledge the messy mix of longing for good and pull toward harm that swims within our hearts, we feel known, and we trust you to lead us.

Paradoxes and tensions do not surface at the start but instead arise in the middle of the journey. At the outset of a trip, our own high hopes and a leader's rallying cries spur us on, and when we finally cross the finish line, we sigh and laugh in grateful contentment. But along the way, bogged down in the swamp of a pandemic or the dark tunnel of a difficult marriage, we need preachers who can name truths with nuance. Insightful observation about the paradoxes of life can fortify us to keep going in the middle of the journey. Let's look at a few examples.

Here are five paradoxes about love. Can you add a sixth?

---

7. Pieper, *Faith, Hope, and Love*, 164.
8. Norris, *Amazing Grace*.
9. Buechner, *Beyond Words*.

1. Love is energizing, and it is exhausting.
2. Love costs us everything, and it gives us everything.
3. When we love one person well, we are learning how to love the many.
4. Sometimes love requires immense effort over many years, and sometimes it floods our hearts instantly and effortlessly.
5. Sometimes the most curmudgeonly people love more deeply than those who seem most kind.
6. Yours: Love _____.

3. Contrast It with Its Opposite

I can't tell you how surprised and thrilled I was to learn that colors had opposites in elementary school. The color wheel placed on my tiny desk was a revelation. I stared in wonder at the genius who had figured this out. Our art teacher proceeded to show us how much better we could see purple when it sat next to yellow, or red when it was next to green. Contrasts clarify. In some realms, such as the directions on a compass, opposites are readily apparent and undebatable. Things are less clear-cut in conceptual domains like virtues and vices. That lets us employ contrasts to play with and propose new facets of a good or an ill. For example, Dallas Willard attempted to clear away muddled thinking on the life of discipleship when he wrote, "Grace is not opposed to effort. It is opposed to earning. Effort is action. Earning is attitude."[10]

Elie Wiesel, quoting others, noted that the opposite of love is not hatred but indifference.[11] When we first hear this, we may object. Technically, the opposite of love is hatred. That is its dictionary antonym. Apathy is but the pale beige to hatred's red. But as we hear Wiesel recount the horrors of the Holocaust made possible by indifferent bystanders, we grasp his point. His contrast both convinces and convicts us, for we can usually dodge the accusation of harboring outright hatred. "Who, us? We are far too nice to be guilty of such an ugly, base emotion." But to the charge of indifference,

---

10. Willard, "Live Life to the Full," 1.

11. Wiesel made this comment in an interview, October 26, 1986, in *US News and World Report*, but its history goes back to a publication in German as early as 1866. https://quoteinvestigator.com/2019/05/21/indifference.

most of us must plead guilty. A contrast sharpens thinking and, in the process, may elicit recognition and repentance as well.

4. Expose Its Roots

The next three stepping stones to fresh articulation trace an agricultural theme. Scripture often uses the language of roots, soil, fruit, and pruning to describe human growth or dilapidation. Skilled gardeners do not merely trim the outer leaves of sprawling weeds; they tunnel to their roots to eliminate them. As experienced pastors, when we see a behavior erupt on the surface, we also do well to ask, "Where did this begin? How far down does this go? What is the poison spring at the source?" The root of a vice could be a subtle lie to which a needy heart has listened. More positively, the starting point of welcoming and growing a virtue could be a space we make within ourselves where we can explore the possibility of being wrong and consider a better way. That space forms a patch of soil where humility can take root. Humility bears the fruit of courage to change.

Vices often get their start in the ground of wounds and lingering traumas, which predispose us to cast about in destructive directions for comfort. The root of a vice pervading a congregation may be a systemic injustice that has plagued its community for generations. When we name those roots in our preaching, we compel our listeners to dig deeper. We invite the Holy Spirit to remove all that is not life-giving within us and expose what is unjust and unholy in our nation, our stewardship of creation, our neighborhood, and our congregational culture.

Ultimately, the root and source of all goodness is God, and we must preach that clearly. We preach virtues on the way to or as an outcome of preaching Christ, who graciously clothes us with them. We pursue virtues avidly while knowing that they are ultimately gifts. We do not earn or achieve faith, hope, or love, nor patience or gentleness. We ask for faith. Sometimes we beg for it, like the boy's father in Mark 9. Faith comes to us as a gift, which means that any faith we muster is cause for humility and gratitude and even wide-eyed wonder when it comes our way.

5. Show Its Ideal Environment

We do not attempt to grow ferns in the desert or a cactus in a rainforest—soil and other environmental factors matter when we want a plant to thrive.

As we mentioned, the ancients understood virtues to grow best in academies and gymnasiums. The saints of the early church understood prayer to flourish where fellow saints gathered to practice it regularly. A healthy corporate culture engenders entrepreneurial risk-taking, and a dysfunctional family is fertile soil for shame, toxic secrecy, and a chronic fear of failure. We preach to cultivate grace-filled communities that offer freedom to risk and to give and receive love. We speak to foster loving homes that honor, celebrate, and nurture each member. We encourage neighborhood cultures of mentoring, where younger people can stretch out in the rich soil of being known, cherished, and believed in by an older person in their lives.

When we consider the soil in which virtues and vices thrive, we attend to the environments we cultivate within our hearts and our communities. Just as we can look at a landscape and predict what will grow well there, we can look at a gathering, listen to the tone of the words spoken there, and guess whether gentleness and joy or shame and mistrust will flourish. While the source is ultimately God, vivid biblical imagery suggests that we nurture growth or thwart it by the lies that we bend our ears towards, the habits and practices we take up or fail to, and the cynicism we consume in our news feed. Preach to sharpen your listeners' awareness of the environments that foster sin or righteousness. As you prepare to preach on money, ask: What is the soil in which greed is most likely to flourish? How are we tilling, fertilizing, and watering that soil through our congregational and individual practices? What is the soil in which generosity and contentment thrive? What activities nurture that?

6. Let Us See Its Fruit over Time

One definition of wisdom is the ability to foresee the long-term consequences of an action. But that is not only an ability; it is also a choice. We often fail to look six steps out from a destructive action we are pondering simply because we do not want to. We want to believe that we are immune from its inevitably painful consequences. Yet, that is how sin entices. It tells us that we can isolate our actions from their formative power on our hearts. But our choices to turn inward, protect ourselves, and refuse to risk love are steadily but inexorably changing our hearts.

I will never forget the sermon I heard where the preacher told the story of family friends who had become obsessed with getting the desired verdict in a property dispute case. The preacher had not seen them for a few years when she visited them, years into their battle. She said, "They were barely recognizable. Their very faces had changed. Hardened. Bitter resolve to gain justice had overtaken all other facets of their lives." By her vivid description of the consequences of steadily cultivating bitterness over time, this preacher was able to call us to let it go without delay.

It can be tough to believe that our small acts of kindness or generosity will bear meaningful fruit over time. We wonder what difference it will make. Your role as a preacher is to show us the shaping power of small yet hard choices that we make to show mercy, practice gentleness in conversation, and offer empathy to family members who annoy you. Paul urged the Philippians to approve what is excellent (Phil 1:10), to be people who could see all that is lovely and life-giving about the gifts God gives.

7. Walk Us through a Process

We are easily overwhelmed at the outset of a complex change process, sometimes so much so that we never set out at all. We feel like we are at the base of Everest, staring up at it, so daunted that we cannot begin. Sermons can serve as the trailside sign that says, "Two miles to the first rest stop." Start here. Take this one small step. That step will encourage and strengthen you to take the next one. We see a stepwise process in Romans 5:3–5, where Paul describes how suffering well produces perseverance, which gives birth to character, which engenders hope. The overarching force animating the whole process is the grace and love of God, but one small step we can take is to embrace our suffering, looking for how it is fortifying us to persevere. God calls us to be hopeful and patient, cheering our hearers on as they start difficult processes.

If you use a car wash, you have probably seen that classic loyalty ploy, the punch card offering you a free car wash after you pay for several. Admittedly, none of them work fabulously, but Chip and Dan Heath cite a study that compared users who were given a card with eight squares to punch vs. those who received a card with ten squares but with the first two already filled in. The same number of punches were required, but those who felt they had a head start ("Lucky you! The first two are already punched!") were nearly twice as likely to complete their cards.[12] So, in addition to mapping out a change process, your next sermon could show us that we are

---

12. Heath and Heath, *Switch*, 97.

already well on the way. "You've taken the first step already! You showed up here today, and Jesus loves to help those who come to him."

8. Name Our Internal Resistances

Some of us are exhausted, and it is hard to make changes or choose the more arduous path when we feel so depleted. What does that mean for us as we preach? First, recognize with empathy that your listeners have endured a lot just by residing on this planet for the past few years. Their reserves for heroic efforts are shot. Others have suffered specific personal trauma, which leaves them wary of authority and cautious about risk. Weariness, disappointment, despair, fear, pride, and shame can make us resist or hesitate to step out in obedience. Naming these with compassion makes us trustworthy.

9. Acknowledge the External Challenges

During the pandemic, hospitality and expressions of love took on radically different shapes. If they were ever popular in your church, holy kisses went into steep decline. But myriad other avenues for expressing love were closed for us, and wise preachers will adjust for that. I heard a sermon mid-pandemic urging us to show hospitality to others (which was indeed the message of the Scripture being preached) with no acknowledgment of the limitations listeners would face in living that out. It failed to resonate for me. The external barriers differ widely from one cultural context to another, so we need to attend carefully to them. Some of us live in countries where our governments are exerting enormous pressure on the running of our congregations. We all live in lands where prevailing cultural messages battle against gospel values and promises. Naming the external barriers is compassionate, and it is strategic. It arms listeners as it forewarns them, and it builds trust as they see that you know what they are facing.

10. Give Us Models

Tell us about the characters in Scripture, history, movies, novels, the news, or your family and friendship circle who modeled love as they made hard choices, turned hard turns, or paid high costs to love. These stories teach as they make abstract concepts concrete. They inspire as they paint attractive pictures that make us desire that life. Stories may open a path we had not seen: show us that more is possible. Carolyn Gordon ends her powerful and wise sermon on Jesus' call to forgive in Matthew 5 with the moving story of Ruby Bridges, who at age six forgave those who sought to block her path as she walked to a formerly segregated school. She concludes, "Sometimes we need models. Ruby can be that model for us."[13]

As you seek to grow as a person of wisdom who preaches virtues and vices effectively, may the fear of the Lord be at the heart of that pursuit (Prov 9:10), and may your journey of growth as a practitioner and teacher of wisdom be marked by joy.

Ask This:

1. Of the ten strategies named above, which comes naturally to me? Which of these strategies have I never tried in my preaching?
2. Can I recall a sermon where, as a listener, I was energized and grew in my understanding because the preacher used one of these strategies? What did he or she do particularly well?

Try This:

1. Pick one of these ten stepping stones and use it in your next sermon to move across the bridge from abstract concept to an idea your listeners can grasp, remember, and put into action.
2. This week, keep a note-taking app handy and be on the lookout for how stories you read on social media, news sites, etc., could illustrate the opposite of a virtue, the environment in which a vice grows, etc. Jot things down, even if they don't fit next week's sermon. Train your mind to see examples of these.

---

13. Gordon, "Fighting the Good Fight," sermon preached for Calvin Symposium on Christian Worship, 2013, https://worship.calvin.edu/resources/resource-library/symposium-2013-forgiveness/.

5

Preacher as Storyteller

Fueling Faith by Narrating the Past

> And beginning with Moses and all the prophets, he explained to them what was said in all the Scriptures concerning himself. They asked each other, "Were not our hearts burning within us while he talked with us on the road and opened the Scriptures to us?"
>
> —LUKE 24:27 AND 32

SEARING PAIN ENGULFED THEM. It fell over the eyes of this pair of disciples. As they trudged toward the little town of Emmaus, they only saw the road right before them. Trauma had split open their world, and no thread and needle could stitch it back together; no platitudes could make sense of their grief and loss. At first, they barely noticed that a third traveler had come alongside them. It is not clear if Jesus deliberately hid his identity from them or if their grief kept them from recognizing him. Either way, they conversed with him as with a stranger, but that did not stop them from pouring out a torrent of dashed hopes and heartaches. He listened. Then they listened—for quite awhile, as Jesus drew them deeper than they may have ever gone into their shared and tangled history, interpreting their ancient texts in the radiant light of his mission and identity. Brittle places inside them melted in the warmth of his presence. The distant past came alive for them, redeeming and healing the recent past as they learned its place within their Creator's vast and cosmic story. As they broke bread together, they saw him clearly at last.

This chapter focuses on how we narrate the past in sermons. Though church history, world history, and our own quirky lives give us rich storehouses of life lessons, we will concentrate on telling the stories of Scripture with lively energy and powerful impact. Preaching that describes our own large and strange family photo album, from Cain to Priscilla, builds the memory of God's past work into the brains and hearts of God's people and uncovers its ongoing resonance with the stories we are living now.

If you use our verb form paradigm as a litmus test of your preaching, you will be asking at this point how well you spoke from the past tense. In preaching, we sometimes say that our task is to "make the Bible come alive for today." This goal has merit but can cause us to envision the word of God as dead, in need of our valiant resuscitation efforts. Conceived another way, we invite listeners to enter the very much alive world of the Scriptures. Whichever way we describe the process, our goal is to tell one living and compelling story.

Talented storytellers naturally blur past and present, shifting into the present tense while they spin out a tale: "But watch what Peter does next!" "Notice Esther's clever strategy here." That shift is fitting; it brings the distant past close. It honors and reflects Scripture's approach to history. Mark's Greek often shifts into present tense as he narrates Jesus' activity.[1] The biblical worldview understands the past as a living, shaping, and highly vocal force that impacts the present. Ellen Davis laments preachers who view the Old Testament as standing "at an immense distance from us . . . across a gulf that is wide and deep."[2] Instead, she insists that our preaching is clothed with power when we experience it as an "*immediate presence* that exercises shaping force in Christian lives—indeed that serves as a source of salutary pressure on our lives."[3] Lively shared memory fuels communities of faithful discipleship, and Scripture portrays forgetting as one of the straightest paths to idolatry. Before we home in on storytelling skills for preaching, let's briefly notice how story and other practices shaped communal memory, to gain a better grasp of how important shared memory is to the vitality of the God's people.

---

1. In roughly 151 places where we would expect a past tense, Mark uses the historical present. See for example Mark 2:8, 4:1, 6:1, and 8:20.

2. Davis, *Wondrous Depth*, 2.

3. Davis, *Wondrous Depth*, 2.

Marking Time, Sacred Space, Embodied Practices

Scripture invites God's people into rich and embodied habits of remembering. God calls his people to sear the past and its meaning upon their hearts through spatial markers such as altars, time markers like festivals, and later the rituals of baptism and Eucharist. As John Hendrix writes, "At the core of *anamnesis* (remembrance) is the capacity to take hold of an event or occurrence from the historical past and to allow that event . . . to take hold of oneself."[4]

Ancient Israel's very landscape, both natural and human-made, bore insistent witness to God's dealings with his people, from the altars Abraham and Jacob made, to the stones the leaders hoisted out of rivers (Exod 28:12; Josh 4:7), to the temple where people encountered and rejoiced in the Lord. As they lifted their eyes to the hills, they remembered to place their faith in God, the source of all help (Ps 120). Their willingness to set apart spaces and mark time with intention cultivated strong shared memories, which in turn shaped and held them.

The ancient Hebrew people did not conceive memory as a static possession, lodged and tucked away in individual brains, the way some of us crammed in the Krebs cycle for a biology test. Instead, they understood remembering to be a lively communal practice that required intentional choices and amply repaid their efforts. A well-nourished memory fed faith in their hearts, equipped them to fight fears and resist idolatry, and fueled them to take risks with courage. Moreover, memory bears the inward fruits of gratitude and humility, dispositions of the heart that naturally turn outward in acts of justice, hospitality, and generosity toward creation and creatures.

The Israelites' marking of time and space was commendable, but an altar is just a pile of stones to a later generation that has not heard why their ancestors built it. Objects and rituals require interpretation. Thus, God urges the Israelites to the even livelier practice of storytelling, narrating God's work to deliver them and their work to make that necessary again and again. The very process of hearing stories and identifying with (or being repulsed by) characters folded later listeners into the family of God like eggs into pancake batter. As they watched God patiently work with Jacob or Naomi or Simon Peter, they learned what God loved and valued and began to imagine God working on their behalf in similar ways.

---

4. Hendrix, "Making the Trip," 420.

When we intentionally and truthfully recall our failings and wounds and God's mercy to us, we position ourselves to receive God's healing work within our hearts and in our relationships with others. As we place those struggles within the biblical narrative, some details get sharper, and others recede into the background, with grace permeating it all. In Joseph's life, after years of gaining perspective, he was able to look back on all that happened to him and say to his brothers, "Even though you intended to harm me, God intended it for good" (Gen 50:20). Gratitude for God's overriding providence in his life made Joseph a fundamentally merciful man. Joseph is a forerunner of the beloved community Christ inaugurated in his radical graciousness towards those who wronged him. Theologian Stanley Hauerwas envisions that community when he writes, "The possibility of reconciled memory between peoples who have wronged and been wronged by one another is but another name for the church."[5] Practices of remembering well together can position us for reconciliation as we hear and tell the truth about the past with honesty and love.

The Scriptures called the Israelites to engage in a courageous and unsettling level of honesty about their humble origins and their history of enslavement. They freely and repeatedly told stories of ancestors who were scoundrels, selling their wives and brothers down the river to protect their hides. The practice of storytelling was a form of confession: "This is who we are. Yes, sadly, it is true—we did this." We can learn a lot from their practice of telling the whole truth about their nation. A community that commits to this uncomfortable practice will gain the humility needed to bridge deep divides. God also wanted humility to mark their relations to other nations and immigrants coming from those nations. The writer of Deuteronomy appealed to the Israelite's past oppression as he called them to show mercy toward sojourners and slaves (Deut 15:12–15; 24:17–18). His fervent hope was that the memories of receiving the hospitality of God would spark lavish generosity toward strangers.

The Power of Story

How do we preach the biblical past so that it fuels lively faith? We tell its stories, and we tell them *as* stories. We don't view narrative texts as cupboards that we can pillage for lists of five principles that start with the letter P or spell out the word DREAM. In God's quest to build the memory of his

5. Hauerwas, "Why Time Cannot Heal," 46.

faithful ways into his people, God could have required that they stand at attention for a daily recitation of the bare facts, with lengthy lists of names and dates. Instead, God urged them to gather around and reenact the divine drama in all its dynamic tension, messiness, and scandal. Why do we love a well-told story so much?

While some stories are so effective at lulling children to sleep that we call them bedtime stories, the deeper reality about stories is their capacity to shock us awake. Far from soothing us, they get under our skin and simultaneously haunt, bother, and delight us. They propel us forward even as they pierce us to the heart, marking us far more indelibly than reciting a list of rules ever could. We find ourselves connecting emotionally with characters, just as David did as he listened with rising anger and empathy to the tale of the man whose lamb was robbed from him.

As we watch characters grow or fail to, we sharpen and clarify our values and strengthen our resolve to bend and stretch as the story we currently live demands. We hope to make the crucial turn like Zacchaeus did, and we desperately wish to avoid the sad path we saw Solomon take. As we see those choices bear either luscious or rotten fruit, we come to love and desire the life-giving fruit. That is part of the magic of stories—they deepen desire for the good even as they sharpen our understanding of it. As you embark on preaching Scripture's stories, keep in mind these three qualities of an effective story.

Effective stories are sneaky. They need to be because the challenging truths we tell will meet with deep resistance. We call people to change in ways that threaten the core of their identity, as individuals or as congregations. If they are paying attention, they will hear us sometimes imply that they are pursuing pathways that lead to death. When we state that directly, people tend to shut down and fold their arms in silent defensiveness. I know I do. Preachers need to tell all the truth, but we often need to come in from an angle. As Emily Dickinson puts it, "Tell all the truth but tell it slant . . . The truth must dazzle gradually, or every man be blind."[6] Think of the moments Jesus had a hard truth to deliver and nimbly said, "Let me tell you a story." Jesus seemed to know that an engrossing parable could sneak past cultural and generational differences and spiritual defenses, as every listener connected with the core emotions and tensions it named and elicited.

---

6. Dickinson, "Tell All the Truth but Tell it Slant," poem 1263, *Complete Poems*.

Effective stories provide distance. We intuitively grasp the truth that stories bring us closer as we gather around an intimate fire to hear them. Their suspenseful plots and striking scenes enthrall us. But they possess a counterintuitive power as well: they can carve out for us a safe, imaginative space, at some remove from our current struggles and confusion. They set us at a mental distance from our pressing realities. This diffuses tension, lowers defenses, and allows us to absorb and ponder a truth together. Theologian Richard Jensen puts it this way:

> Distance and participation are helpful words to use to describe listener involvement in story preaching. Distance creates a certain kind of safety. David was at a distance from his situation as he listened to Nathan's story. In the safety of this distance, we often participate deeply in the story that is told, hearing things about ourselves that we might not otherwise be able to hear. Distance enables participation. The aim of story preaching is to create a world in story which is safe enough for people to enter and powerful enough to involve the hearer in personal participation in words of judgment and grace.[7]

The magic of distance is that intimate participation happens within the safety of the story space. We engage, not at arm's length but wholeheartedly, and we find ourselves moved, sometimes with deep conviction and sometimes with delight.

Effective stories teach. A strange thing happens to some of us on the way to a seminary degree. We get a head full of abstract concepts that we must share, and because they fascinate us so much, we assume our listeners will devour them as well. As a result, we come to think of stories as mere illustrations of those truths, with little intrinsic capacity to teach. We may even feel a little guilty about how much we enjoy preaching the narratives of Scripture since we believe that they are a side dish or perhaps dessert, but not the main course.

Ray Anderson describes how the very presence of red letters in his Bible formed his thinking as a child. The teachings of Jesus were the heart of it in his understanding; the stories of his miracles were mere backdrops recorded to authenticate that teaching. He reflects, "Only later did I come to understand that what Jesus *did* was as authoritative and as much revelation of God as what he said and taught. When Jesus healed on the Sabbath,

---

7. Jensen, *Telling the Story*, 138–39.

the act of healing became a text by which a true theology of the Sabbath was revealed."[8]

Five Skills of Storytelling

As you preach your delight in stories, trust that they are teaching even as they hopefully also delight your listeners. They are revealing the character of God even as they teach us how to be human. And trust the Holy Spirit to say different things through the same story. The open-ended nature of the narrative medium gives it agility, enabling the Spirit to speak timely and specific words to various people. Since stories carry so much power to convict, connect, teach, and transform, let's work hard at the practical skills of telling stories well.

1. Get Up Close with Your Characters

The characters we meet in Scripture can seem utterly remote from our experience. For instance, they hand each other sandals to seal a marriage deal (Ruth 4:8) or bake their bread using excrement as fuel for the oven (Ezek 4:12). But at the core, they are distressingly (and comfortingly) just like us. They agonize over the future, they grow, and then they backtrack. Some of them, like Jacob, soften and bend balletically toward grace as their years unfold. Some harden and hunker down in their bentness toward evil, like Pharaoh and King Herod. But in the biblical story world, few characters stay the same, and everybody matters. Eugene Peterson notes how remarkable it is, in contrast to other ancient Near Eastern historical accounts, that so many minor characters in Scripture get names and crucial parts to play in the history of Israel. He writes,

> Because they were convinced that God was working among them where they were, each day, they believed what they did, whether in faith or unbelief, sin or righteousness, obedience or rebellion, was significant. Because it was significant, it was capable of being narrated *as a story*, that is, as an account in which what people did had consequences and was part of a structured purpose.... Everything in it has a point, a meaning. Nothing is irrelevant. Each character, however minor, plays a part.[9]

8. Anderson, *Shape of Practical Theology*, 12.
9. Peterson, *Five Smooth Stones*, 80.

Preacher as Storyteller

One of the pitfalls of preaching the villains of Scripture is that we dismiss them too quickly, caricaturing them in ways that cause our listeners to distance themselves from them precisely when a closer look would cause a potent moment of recognition. If we want our listeners to come to see their tendencies toward legalism and hypocrisy, then we had better not attack the Pharisees from the outset. Instead, let's treat them with sympathy, naming their fears, honorable intentions, and devotion to Israel and Israel's God so that we can get close enough to them that they can hold up mirrors for our reactive tendencies. Your goal is to look out at the world *with* your characters, understanding their motives and desires. Otis Moss helps us empathize with King David as he slides into adultery and murder by imagining some of the wounds that may have made him vulnerable to such behavior.

> David's gaze is cast against the stone skyline of the kingdom. . . . . His father never believed he could lead . . . until the day the prophet showed up, and a wide vision was cast through the narrow window of Bethlehem. . . . He is king now, but he cannot erase the light ache in his heart. He will always be the boy from Bethlehem, the little barrio shepherd with country ways, who could not erase the stench of wool and manure from his skin. As he continues to look across the horizon of his city, his eyes rest upon a rooftop. The sun dances across the black skin of a woman bathing in a tiny tub. Not realizing his mouth was slightly opened, he imagines his next campaign as he stares.[10]

Now, some might object that Moss is speculatively interjecting emotions and motivations into the text, with his description of the ache in David's heart. We do want to be somewhat cautious about assuming too much. We can signal that we are extrapolating, as Moss deftly does throughout his sermon, by adding a phrase like, "I wonder if he felt . . ." or, "It may have been hard for him to . . ." The African American preaching tradition often brings the lovely phrase, "In my sanctified imagination I see (David gazing . . .)."

Make friends with your characters, even the ones who get on your nerves. Ask them tough questions. Sarah, what did you most fear at that moment? Hagar, what did you most deeply desire? Jonah, what did it feel like to finally admit who you were to the sailors in the storm? Members of the crowd, why did you turn so sharply in your hearts as you listened to

---

10. Moss, *Blue Note Preaching*, 28.

Jesus? (Luke 4:30). Who helped you? What blocked you? What did you see, and to what were you blind? What did it cost you to say yes to Jesus? What was at stake?

Sometimes in our preaching about characters in Scripture, we settle for preaching *them* and not the gospel they reveal. We preach them as morality tales, dispensers of object lessons for our lives. We close the sermon by encouraging listeners to be more like—or nothing like—this character, and we fail to root that appeal in a robust proclamation of the grace of God, as God's redeeming action in the story has displayed it. Sometimes that work is veiled, such as in the book of Esther, but we must always seek to discern the hand and the ways of God and highlight it.

2. Paint Vivid Sets for Your Story's Scenes

The plot of a play or novel unfolds one scene at a time, with each one introducing a new tension. Each scene grants us a sharper glimpse of a character's true nature and propels us forward to the next scene. A well-crafted opening scene draws listeners into the story. As preacher and homiletician Alyce McKenzie puts it, "Like an extroverted host, a scene invites us to come into the house rather than stand out on the porch looking in. . . . Scenes make spectators into participants."[11]

Scenes generally take place in one physical setting. In depicting that setting, staged or filmed scenes have a visual advantage over novels or sermons. But we bring one advantage. When we paint the location with vivid language, a wide variety of listeners can create the scene in their imaginations, adapting it to the cultural referents that spring most readily to mind based on their diverse lived experiences.

Practitioners of *Lectio Divina* encourage us to enter the scenes of the stories in Scripture imaginatively as a form of prayer. Ignatius of Loyola invited disciples to engage all the senses as they prayerfully read Scripture. One *lectio* practice involves gathering people to read Scripture aloud, asking what they would have seen if they had been one of the characters that day. Then listeners hear it again, inquiring about sounds, then tastes, then sensations on the skin, and even smells. The idea with this slow, repetitive process is to provoke some of the gifts of memory we discussed above, letting the past come alive in the present as the story washes over us and seeps beneath our skin. We can offer our listeners a taste of the delightfulness

---

11. McKenzie, *Making a Scene*, 4–5.

of *lectio* when we paint vivid scenes that engage multiple senses. Watch how McKenzie does that here with crisp sentence fragments as she begins a sermon on the first chapter of the Gospel of Mark.

> The smell of martyrs' blood mingled with the dirt of the coliseum floor. The sounds of flames licking at the buildings as Rome burned. A wild glint in an emperor's eyes. The taste of bread and wine as they share their holy meal, but their hands tremble as they reach out to receive it. This is the Gospel of Mark. Probably written at the outset of a persecution. It's written in a crucible: this accounts for its high blood pressure, urgent feel, for its stress on sacrifice, for its terse language. There is not much time; there is lots of danger. Persecutions are imminent. Are you in, or are you out?[12]

We write with *visual* descriptions on our minds, ignoring taste, touch, scent, and sound. But for stories to do their work and spark our imaginations, our sermons must engage multiple senses.

3. Slice Open a Moment and Linger There

Talented storytellers sound like the seven-year-old who bursts in the door having just discovered tadpoles at the nearby creek and who urgently needs a bucket and our help to collect them. *Right now*. Their words tumble out at a furious pace, adding liveliness and immediacy to the telling. If we can follow along, we love it. But crucially, skilled tellers of tales also know how to slow way down when it matters. The Gospel of Mark gallops forward breathtakingly for much of its plot. But then it lingers, narrating in detail the final days of Jesus' life, asking us to pause and absorb those brutal final exchanges at the trial, the beating and mocking, the moments of cowardice and outright betrayal from the disciples, and finally the agony of the crucifixion. Frankly, we would all rather fast-forward to the resurrection—and much Protestant spirituality does just that. Whether we are the teller or the hearer, those slow moments make us uncomfortable, and on some level, with biblical stories, we know the outcome already, so why dwell on those awkward times?

We linger at the points of tension because they are where listeners' lives are won or lost. They, too, face temptations to compromise that play out over days, much more than split-second heroic moments. When we tell the story of Joseph running from Potiphar's wife, we tend to home in on

12. McKenzie, *Novel Preaching*, 63.

the critical moment when he ran and left his cloak. Still, the scene played out over several days that were no doubt filled with tension, temptation, resistance, and most likely some entertaining of enticing options. Let's wade into those murky waters rather than resolve the pressure too quickly. Let's preach that past in the present tense. What is at stake? What will it cost him to flee? Show us that you have lived in the places of tension your characters and listeners inhabit.

Not all tension is caused by a looming catastrophe. Pressure can enter our lives when we hear happy news, such as the promise of a promotion, if that news requires us to weigh four dozen competing values as we respond to it. The job upgrade involves a move, which threatens to throw off everything. Whether hard or happy, this news is called the inciting incident in a narrative, and it always pushes the character off-balance. It sets in motion everything that follows. Often in Scripture, none other than God messes everything up, throwing ordered lives into chaos as God sends them on ridiculous-sounding quests, asks them to bear scorn as they build arks, or compels them to drastically cut their fighting forces. "The Lord said to Abram, "Go . . . to the land that I will show you." The angel said to Mary, "Blessed are you among women!" Those words upset the equilibrium of the characters' lives.

As most stories begin, the main character lives life in balance. Maybe it is not happy, but it is basically under control. Then an event occurs that swings it out of balance. It reveals desires, fears, and flaws and sends the character on a quest to fulfill the promise. If we who preach their stories are willing to walk alongside them, lingering especially at the hinges where they made their most challenging choices, we will find that their stories bend outwards to us. They shine an uncomfortable but curiously transformative light upon our own.

4. Sneak in Historical Background and Exegetical Insights

History as a discipline has a bad rap. We think of high school history classes and yawn, remembering long, dull sessions memorizing lists of presidents or kings and their battles. But what if history took the form of epic adventures with riveting plot twists? As Rudyard Kipling mused, "If history were told in the form of stories, it would never be forgotten." As we noted earlier, stories can sneak up on us in the realm of conviction, but they have another nimble capacity. They allow us to smuggle our exegetical work in, cunningly tucked inside attractive packages. While writing a sermon about Hannah's encounter with Eli, the priest, where he accused her of drunkenness, I learned that the Hebrew word for "drunk" could also mean "full." That is an interesting fact, but where does it fit in a sermon? I slipped it in on her lips, creating a sermon in the first person where Hannah began her story this way:

> He thought I was drunk! Eli, the priest, did. He was watching me pour out my heart to God, and he thought I was drunk. And that's kind of a bitter joke because the word drunk means full in my language—someone is too full of wine. And the irony was, I was praying there that day, not because I was full, but because I was *so empty*. You might know what it feels like to live with an emptiness inside, a silent ache that won't go away.

That opening begins to bring the past into the present. It taps a resonance with empty places within all of us. The sermon tapped that more as it progressed. Another way we bring the past into the present is to update the biblical image, with a quick aside mid-story, where we compare an unfamiliar feature to a modern equivalent. The week I was preaching on the shepherd who left the ninety-nine sheep to go after the one, Thai divers were working around the clock to rescue boys trapped in a cave. I quickly referenced that vivid current story, which thankfully had just ended happily. It was a dynamic equivalent that shone a light on the mentality and commitment of a shepherd, even for city-dwelling listeners who had never watched one at work.

The bottom line here is that every piece of exegetical material you want to include in a sermon weighs the sermon down a little, so it must earn its fare. If you find the history you learn about fascinating, your next task is to articulate *why*—and why that matters for *this* sermon. A compelling answer should spring readily to mind, as in, "Because Hannah was the very opposite of full! And many listeners are coming empty this Sunday." "Because shepherds don't just abide in their fields like statues in a Christmas Eve tableau; they climb rocks and risk injury to rescue the vulnerable. I want them to know that Jesus Christ does that for us today." If you cannot articulate that it is just an interesting fact that does not drive the sermon forward. Perhaps it is a candidate for smuggling in another time, but it is not worth the cost this time.

5. Vary Event Sequencing

One more note on that Hannah sermon. It caught listeners' attention to begin it with the five-word sentence, "He thought I was drunk!" Listeners did not know who "he" was or even who was speaking. From there, I had to do some fast backtracking. I had jumped into the middle of the story, deliberately entering it at a point of heightened dramatic tension between Hannah and the priest. Sometimes called *in medias res* (in the middle of things), this technique captures a strong emotion within the plot from the outset. It intentionally sacrifices clarity for the sake of intrigue. Clarity may dawn slowly or suddenly over the following few lines, but it should come relatively soon in a narrative sermon of this sort. Listeners will lose patience if they remain confused too long. Especially in a first-person narrative such as this one, where listeners are already thrown off-center by the sermon's unusual form, it was essential to name Eli in the following sentence and for another character to call Hannah by name a moment later.

While our natural tendency is to narrate from start to finish in chronological order, we have a lot of freedom to vary the sequencing of a story. We can even change the narrator's distance in time from the entire story. For example, Rev. Jeff Frymire began a sermon as if he were a disciple looking back from two decades beyond the event in his passage. He launched with this simple but striking line: "I have never looked at bread in the same way again." This line drew us in and allowed him to tell afresh the familiar story of the little boy who brought his lunch to Jesus, narrating it as a man who became a house church leader, looking back on that day.[13]

Memory fuels faith, and we fill the fuel tanks of memory by the practices we engage in, individually and communally. For example, we set apart seasons and physical spaces and practice the rituals of baptism and the Lord's Supper to stoke the fires of memory. But I would argue that our most crucial task as we lead to foster lively and faithful communal memory is to tell the stories of Scripture well. That will interpret, deepen, and amplify those potent but mute physical and temporal markers. I call it a task, but that word can obscure the happy reality that storytelling is delightful—for hearers and tellers. So, commit yourself to the ministry of telling Scripture's stories well, and may you delight in it.

---

13. Frymire, sermon preached at Fuller Theological Seminary, 2007.

Ask This:

- Who are your favorite storytellers? What makes them so compelling and enjoyable?
- Do you think of yourself as a gifted storyteller? Is it something you enjoy? If not, what would need to change for you to answer in the affirmative?

Try This:

- Pick an obscure character and give them the microphone for all or a portion of a sermon. Tell the story of Naaman, the leprous commander of the Syrian army, from the perspective of the servant girl who gets the action going. Tell the story of the lost sheep from the perspective of the one out in the wild. Tell us about Esther from the perspective of the eunuch who prepares her to go before the king.
- Challenge your scene-painting skills by portraying a scene in vivid detail but using only one sensory descriptor. For example, walk us through the narrative of Jairus and the woman with the flow of blood, describing it in vivid detail but only by way of the odors we would have smelled if we had been there.

6

Preacher as Priest

Discerning the Work of God in the Present

"What if, in scrubbing dead bugs off whitewall tires at the youth carwash, in summoning the energy to listen attentively to a troubled couple, and in focusing on a column of figures at a finance meeting, we were alert to the workings of Divine Wisdom in our hands, our ears, our eyes? For one thing, it would make us better teachers and preachers. Being constantly alert to the activity of God in the most minuscule of circumstances is a spiritual discipline that is absolutely crucial to communicating God's good news."

—ALYCE MCKENZIE

"I WONDER WHAT GOD is up to now." Jack's eyes would twinkle under their bushy brows as he posed this question to anyone in earshot. It was his response to all sorts of news, from reports of conflict within the church he pastored to good or disturbing global events. As a member of his congregation, I often sidled up to him with distressing news, wanting him to share my outrage or anxiety. Instead, he would calmly breathe out this question. His tranquility irked me to no end. I wanted to shout, "Did you *not hear* what I just said? Why are you not panicking about this?" But I came to appreciate his disciplined practice of holy curiosity and even attempted to imitate it. His question reframed the discussion from fearful reaction to prayerful response, from damage control to discernment of the mysterious work of the risen Christ in our midst.

Jack was like a wide-awake watcher striding along the wall of an old city—not prowling for enemies so much as eagerly awaiting good news. He was ever on the lookout for the activity of the Holy Spirit in the present moment and could ask his favorite question because he knew God well. Jack was steeped in God's word and had walked with God for decades, so he could recognize patterns—he knew what the Holy Spirit was *always* up to—redeeming, healing, suffering with, and sustaining her beloved children through the hardest of times. Jack knew God to be trustworthy to the core, so he could entertain the possibility that in a given dismal crisis his faithful, playful, and endlessly creative God was flipping scripts, twisting plots, and bringing about a much better outcome than Jack could have engineered or imagined on his own.

Every time he asked this question, Jack was preaching to me. Asking it was an act of faith on his part. Asking it *out loud* was an act of leadership. Jack was modeling for me a way of looking out at the world with calm curiosity and vibrant faith. Crucial to Jack's response is how it opened a space in which to listen both to God and people. It was an intrinsically humble stance, and when asked aloud in his context (a small church deeply committed to shared discipleship), it formed a profoundly communal outlook. Like Jehoshaphat, he did not know the answer, so he was inviting others into lively moments of musing together in the presence of the Lord.

Preaching in the present tense refers to the moments in sermons when we ask the timeless yet timely, ancient yet active word of God to resonate with current personal, political, and congregational events. We participate in the Spirit's dance of artfully traversing the distance between the biblical past and the present. As Lischer put it, "No one communicates from some airless, context-free environment, because there is no such thing, and we should never pretend that there is. Those who try to preach in a timeless manner are doomed to reach no one in particular."[1] Present-tense preaching that attends to context involves much more than having a clever take on the latest news or subtly showing how a particular political leader is just like Herod or the Pharaoh we read about in our text today. You do not need a book to help you get better at that—you can do cynical all by yourself, though I hope you will choose not to.

---

1. Lischer, *Just Tell the Truth*, x.

Instead, we plunge into the more profound and more challenging work of interpreting the times with our communities so we may respond to them with radical love. We use the present tense to dare to posit how God may yet be at work in troubling events around us and to make the audacious claim that the Spirit speaks through the Scriptures to us, right here, right now. With the present tense, we ponder what the life of discipleship looks like around our table, on our Zoom calls, at our school. While we want to guard against collapsing the distance too quickly between our world and that of the ancient world, if we are too intimidated by that distance, we will perceive it as an uncrossable chasm and fail to let the word address us today.

If we want to preach with power and resonance in the present tense, we will need to cultivate the habit of tirelessly asking Jack's question—and a few variations of it. Like most of our beneficial practices, this one does not come naturally. We did not clamor to brush our teeth after dinner at age four. The habit became ingrained in us through *practice*. Similarly, during challenging moments, we may need to be intentional about pausing to ask these questions instead of succumbing to reactions that come more naturally, such as pronouncing, denouncing, despairing, or burrowing into a couch with a giant bowl of butter-drenched popcorn. Those practices may feel helpful, but they are, at best, temporary fixes. The discipline of stepping back to see the bigger picture will bear better fruit. It will prepare us to lead well through our preaching. When we ask the questions this chapter introduces, we ideally do so not in solitude but with the communities we love.

Discernment is priestly work. Many Protestants place little value on the role of a priest in the church's life today. We are grateful that Jesus Christ, our great high priest, has done the ultimate priestly work of bearing our sins. Beyond that, we are less clear about an ongoing need for priests. Let's reach further back and consider a critical task of ancient priests. They compelled the people to stop their work and take up odd practices that brought their ancient story into the present. It cannot have always been popular to be the one cajoling folks to leave the market where sales were going exceedingly well and sit in a booth covered in palm leaves for a few days to mark *Sukkot*, the Festival of Booths. Or to pack up the fussy kids and trek over to Jerusalem to offer sacrifices and confess sins, even if those days did end in feasting. The priests persisted in calling people to these disruptive practices because they anchored them in their history, turned them to God in prayer, and invited them into new ways of living in the present. That sounds a lot like the work a pastor does on the Lord's Day.

Let's consider four variations on Jack's core question, each of which will equip you to preach the gospel in the context of present realities.

1. (I Wonder) What Is God up to Now, within Us?

Discernment happens best when we work from the inside out. We too often skip the step of asking how God may be using an event in our home or in the world to refine and grow us, but doing so bears good fruit.

Within Us in Our Struggles

At its core, preaching and pastoral leadership teach people to suffer well. Hardship is inevitable but learning to respond well is the work of a lifetime. Pain always puts us at risk because adversity surfaces the most challenging questions about God's power and love and the most vexing questions about our identity and purpose. Suffering makes us vulnerable to turning away from God in bitterness and gravitating toward behaviors that numb our pain. Ideally, suffering serves as the forge in which we become fearless, free from idols, and fit for fierce battles and essential kingdom work. When it works as hoped, it is where our most profound transformation happens—though rarely on our timetable. When we are slogging through that slow and messy middle, a word from beyond our echo chamber can go a long way toward enabling us to endure.

The author of Hebrews sought to bring just that kind of word in a book many consider to be an extended sermon to a group that was struggling. The writer highlighted the bigger story of how God was at work through their sufferings. Read this sentence aloud three times slowly: "Endure hardship as a discipline; God is treating you as sons and daughters" (Heb 12:7). Can you hear the promise that follows the command? God is in this pain; your loving God is parenting, growing, and shaping you. Hardship is not pleasant, the writer acknowledges, but if you let it, it can indelibly imprint upon you your identity as God's beloved child, and it will bear the fruit of righteousness and peace.

As we preach the news of God at work in our challenges, our verbs will naturally shift into a subset of the present tense, the present progressive. "God *is treating* you as sons and daughters." It's an ongoing process. The power in the present progressive lies in its capacity to acknowledge that we are on the way; we have not arrived. We are learning, but much is still unclear. We are becoming stronger, but we falter. We are growing, but still so far from where we want to be.

Watch how Ellen Davis shifts into the present-progressive tense, evoking the ongoing process that the life of discipleship entails, as she invites listeners to embrace suffering in this Good Friday sermon:

> Walking in the way of the cross—what does that really look like on the ground? [This] is the basic movement of the whole Christian life. But what does that mean in concrete terms, on an ordinary day in the life of any of us? Simply this: walking in the way of the cross is opening yourself to the pain that comes to you, in whatever measure it comes—not looking for pain, not accepting it without question or protest, but rather living with pain honestly and generously, living in a way that gives hope to others.[2]

We humans can bear a surprising amount of pain when we know it has a purpose. Sometimes that purpose is for another, such as the pain mothers endure to bring a child into the world or the minor pain a blood donor endures to serve another in need. But often, that purpose is located squarely within us, as it forges empathy and endurance in our hearts. We preachers invite people to see the work of God and the invitations of God in their present suffering. We get at that in our sermons when we ask questions like:

- How is this struggle inviting you to lean into trust in God?
- In this situation that seems so out of control, what agency do you have to respond creatively?
- What fruit of the Spirit are you asking God to grow in this messy soil?
- For what, even in this hard season, can you give thanks? Who and what has helped you?
- What glimpses of grace are you seeing?

Like the priests of ancient Israel, who invited people to pause and reflect on God's faithfulness in their most challenging times, we preach to help people discern the formative work God is doing within them in their struggles.

---

2. Davis, *Wondrous Depth*, 155.

Preacher as Priest

Within Us, as We Respond to Societal Events

As preachers, it is intuitive to ask what God is doing within us in various personal struggles, from financial or vocational to relational rifts or physical ailments. But when it comes to world events, national political upheaval, violence, and injustice in our streets, we assume that our task is to turn our speech outward, decrying injustice and calling us to act as advocates and allies with those who are suffering. And that is true, but I invite you to pause and take a preliminary step. As we watch political events unfold, our guts react with an array of feelings, begging us to pronounce and vilify. When unsettling events seem to occur at twice the speed we can absorb, we preachers can be quick to declare what a given moment means, what an outrage it is, and with whom we should be outraged. Though that has the veneer of courage, it is actually the easiest and rarely the most productive task. What listeners need in these moments may not be a prophet who declares their conception of truth on God's behalf so much as a priest who bears global and societal pain and carries it to God.

We who lead are rightly eager to figure out how to respond to current events in ways that foster justice, but that work will go better when we attend first to what is surfacing within us as we react to the news. We then ask God to sift what is unproductive or destructive within us and cultivate what moves us towards empathy and peace. This inner work is crucial and primary for pastors and for people who seek to advocate for justice, since it is so easy for that endeavor to become tinged with self-righteous anger and pettiness. We must constantly ask, "What needs to be purified within me? What will it look like for me to honor and listen well to those with whom I disagree?"

Whether it is a contentious election cycle or a polarized debate around immigration, every preacher needs to be asking, "I wonder, amid this global or national event, what God is up to in the people I lead and in me? And perhaps especially, within those with whom I vehemently disagree?" In any politically charged event, some will feel immediate compassion for those in one part of the story, while others will feel sympathy for another. The gospel teaches us to cultivate compassion for both sides and not to take sides quickly or easily. Rather, we are learning to ask what gift those who interpret an event differently can offer us and what truths they can teach us. This will lead to preaching that frames an issue with less stridency and more nuance.

Within Us in Our Church's Struggles

We will at times need to address a pivotal and confusing event in the congregation's life—a sudden staff upheaval, a deep divide over an ethical issue, or a shared tragedy. The pandemic was a global event, but the abrupt move it triggered from gathered to online worship (or no shared worship, in many majority world settings) rippled out, causing thousands of painful local congregational events. They formed part of what Nadia Bolz Weber called "a pandemic of human disappointments."[3] Abrupt closures of physical spaces upended cherished patterns of doing life together. There were a few unexpected gains, but let's face it, myriad heartrending losses.

I suspect that the way pastors narrated and interpreted that shift made a big difference in how congregations weathered it. Did they help us be on the lookout for the gift within the loss? What prayerful practices did they call us to take up? Did they tell the story entirely as an ordeal we were slogging through, biding our time until we could get back to normal, or did they encourage us to keep our eyes open for how we could embrace the struggles of the season and still flourish in it? Did they celebrate the ways people who had been on the margins could now more fully participate in worship services? Are they exploring how to foster a greater ongoing connection with those people, and pondering aloud how this hard season might launch us into more fruitful ministry?

One of Tod Bolsinger's core convictions about times of turbulence in congregations is that they are gifts from God, meant for our growth and our thriving. He urges leaders to believe and insistently give voice to the conviction that "God is taking us into uncharted territory to transform us."[4] I dare you to say that simple sentence out loud in meetings or sermons three times this month. Keeping that perspective front and center will let us focus on discerning and embracing the work of God within us rather than on merely controlling the damage or being the last staff member standing in the latest congregational turbulence.

2. (I Wonder) What Is God up to Now through Us?

When we have done the inner work of bringing our pain into God's presence and letting our hot-take reactions to events surface and be purified, we can

---

3. Bolz Weber, Twitter, March 12, 2020.
4. Bolsinger, *Canoeing the Mountains*, 217.

turn to consider what God might be up to through us as faith communities. Jack's church got a chance to ponder that question in earnest when a car belonging to one of their members was stolen right off the street in front of their home. While not brand new or high-end, it was far from a clunker on its way to the scrap heap. The thief was found, and they knew that pressing charges could lead to his incarceration. So instead, they chose to build a relationship with the man who had taken the car. They met with him to listen to the struggle that had driven him to steal. They heard his genuine sorrow over his rash action. They met his family and learned about their desperate needs. The core members met to pray and take their best shot at answering how God might be at work through them, patiently kneading the question that had guided and enlivened their community like yeast in the dough for many years. Finally, they concluded that they would give the family the car and pool their money to help their family member purchase a similar one. It turns out that Jack's irritatingly insistent question had steadily built into his community the capacity to respond with agility and grace.

The decision was not even particularly hard for them, schooled as they were in a way of seeing that led rather naturally to this course of action. Moreover, it was downright fun—and a fresh wind of lighthearted joy blew through their church as they settled on this decision.

Samuel Wells describes that process this way:

> In our recessional hymn, the choir and . . . members set out to begin the week to come, taking the sacred actions and words and seeking to speak and hear and practice and receive them in every moment of every day. At this moment, the pastor is inviting the eager members of the congregation in their different ways to locate and discern and cherish the place where (the Word) lands and at the next service to bring back the wisdom and wonder of how they met God there.[5]

Many churches, including my own, sprang into action in beautiful and creative ways during the pandemic, delivering meals and communion elements, getting their seniors connected for digital church, calling those most isolated, and hosting online prayer meetings. Homiletician Ahmi Lee describes the role of the pastor in these moments. "The preacher acts as an interpretive leader who . . . discerns with the church God's action in the

---

5. Wells, "Teaching Eucharist."

present moment for the church to join in."⁶ It is a joy to be at the helm of a group of energized, committed disciples in such times.

3. (I Wonder) What Is God up to Now around Us?

We discussed the need to examine our hearts before pronouncing when we learn of tragedies and injustices at the local, national, and international levels. This inward turn prepares us for faithful, disciplined speech when we turn outward. And we must do so eventually because we seek to equip our listeners to do the work of interpretation as they read the news or consume other media. They need to be able to ferret out the underlying values that animate or deaden their society. Hopefully, we are not the only faithful voices they are heeding, but we need to be part of the team, enabling them to frame injustices and suffering in the light of biblical ideals and narratives. While I caution against pastors pronouncing in polarizing ways, we are called to speak the truth about injustices that harm humans and all creation. Sometimes we must do so on frighteningly short notice. We cannot turn our sanctuaries into worship bubbles, highly insulated from the realities of our world. Some moments in our national or global life are so painful, alarming, or egregious that we must lament them the very next Sunday.

Here is the unfortunate truth: as a pastor, you will rarely articulate those moments in a way that satisfies every listener present. Homiletician Frank Thomas puts the dilemma well. "The preacher will never exhaust the meaning or varied ways of looking at a particular situation that may call forth the preacher's address. Thus, addressing a topic of concern assumes both a risk and a wager. The preacher never names reality in moments where all i's can be dotted, and t's crossed."⁷ I have cringed hearing pastors get this wrong, and I have gotten it wrong myself. I do so by silence as often as by rash overreach. We rarely go wrong when we simply express our sorrow and empathy and voice a prayer for all who are hurting. The intentionally tentative, inquisitive tone in an "I wonder" statement could also help us avoid an overly strident certainty.

For example, in the United States, pastors have struggled to weigh in on our many instances of police brutality, especially against African American people. That seems straightforward, but it becomes complicated

---

6. Lee, *Preaching God's Grand Drama*, 147.
7. Thomas, *Exodus Preaching*, 4.

when faithful and long-serving police officers of various ethnicities or their widows and widowers are seated in the pews. Those settings challenge us to honor the best intentions and deepest fears of all present and to express compassion for the silent suffering of numerous folks, present in our pews or not. We must also do more than comfort—we advocate for change where systemic injustices are causing that suffering. That may involve implicating listeners in uncomfortable forms of complicity or gently but clearly exposing their callous indifference.

This work is hard, and no advice I could offer you will make it easy. But Jack's question can help. When we approach our preaching against injustice with the hopeful, curious stance of what God might be up to in the world, we are on the lookout for in-breakings of grace, which subtly changes our preaching. We lament and speak the truth about injustice, but we also highlight the stories of those who are engaging in risky acts of care for creation or solidarity with refugees. We celebrate those who are bravely coming alongside those experiencing homelessness or bringing mental health resources to victims of violence. Finally, we let those stories point us to Jesus Christ, who lived and lives as a healer and redeemer.

4. (I Wonder) What Is the Enemy up to Now?

While Jack's question irked me at first, I came to love the spiritual discipline of asking what God might be up to now. But God is not the only powerful actor at work in our globe, our congregation, or in my heart. The Enemy is also nimbly, skillfully, and persistently at work in every season. We saw in chapter 4 that a deep knowledge of the vices arms us to notice and reject them as they creep into our thoughts, speech, and actions. Similarly, we are better armed when we know that the source of every evil, the bitter enemy of our faith, is hard at work. Satan kicks into high gear in times of transition and turbulence, especially when the church mobilizes to act faithfully in those times.

One of the most obvious things our Adversary is up to is turning our hearts to trust idols and our minds to believe lies. As we noted above, suffering can deepen our faith in the realm of personal pain. We can emerge stronger from those seasons, with a more profound ability to empathize with others, a clarified purpose, and grateful hearts for God's deliverance. But long seasons of pain always put us at risk. The prophets knew how vulnerable Israel was to the comfort and cures put forth by the peddlers of idols. The prophets refused to give false promises or quick fixes when the path to a better future was unclear. Instead, they went into overdrive to root Israel's identity in God in those precarious times. They did so by honestly naming the struggles, by lavish declarations of God's love for God's people, and by the fierce, clear denunciation of the emptiness of idolatry. Their clarity about the work of the enemy to deceive allowed them to sound a note that resonated deeply with the hearts of those still seeking God.

What about Relevance?

In a chapter on preaching with present-tense power about current realities, it may seem odd that the word *relevance* has not yet surfaced. I am all for relevance—I want our sermons to connect with the lives of our listeners and the current realities of our globe. But just as cumin can overtake the flavor of chili, relevance clamors to dominate. A desperate quest for that fast-moving target we call relevance can land us in treacherous territory as preachers.

At its least problematic, the hunt for it is simply distracting. I have instead leaned into the language of discernment. While relevance can feel like an elusive carnival prize that we struggle desperately every week to win, the word *discernment* evokes an active yet peaceful practice, undertaken in the Lord's presence, done communally and on behalf of a faithful community. Wise understanding emerges from curiosity about what we observe, followed by dialogue with faithful others and prayerful thought, all done in deep conversation with Scripture. As we drill down to the bedrock values that are in tension and on display within a given current event, that process will naturally bear the fruit of our words being genuinely relevant.

That sounds like a ponderous process, like one Tolkien's Ent, Treebeard, would undertake at frustratingly slow speed. But those schooled in it can connect the past and present with agility, as Jack's church did with the stolen car. On the preaching front, we see Peter do this in Acts 2. A strange event was confounding the crowds. They were beginning to misinterpret it and thus were at risk of missing the glorious reality unfolding before them. With minimal time for sermon preparation, Peter reached deftly into his bag of biblical narratives and found the words of the prophet Joel. By the power of the Holy Spirit, Peter brought to bear a passage from roughly eight hundred years earlier, demonstrating its timeliness and capacity to decode the present moment. Peter could preach this quintessentially relevant sermon because he engaged in Spirit-filled and Scripture-saturated discernment. While I prefer to invite you to practice discernment over pursuing relevance, it does convey a quality we hope for in sermons. Relevance in preaching implies a sermon that does two things well: it helps us live out our faith and it demonstrates awareness of current realities.

When a sermon is relevant in the word's best sense, it offers concrete, practical steps listeners can take. Listeners want preachers to show them how to live out biblical truth in the coming week. They are grateful when preachers show them a straightforward step to respond to the gospel, even if it is counterintuitive or hard. We who preach want to make Sunday meet this coming Tuesday, knowing what our listeners will face at school, home, and work that week.

Listeners also rightly want preachers to demonstrate that they have an ear to the ground for what is happening locally and globally—that they were not locked away in their study all week. They know about devastating hurricanes six thousand miles away, violence and economic hardship two miles away, and severe losses right within the congregation that week. They are not only aware, but truly troubled by it and able to speak a gospel word that mobilizes the community to give generously, advocate, and care for those affected by such events. Not only must Sunday meet this coming Tuesday, but it must interpret last Tuesday when our listeners come to church grieving and perplexed by what happened then in our nation or hometown. It must turn their hearts to prayer and mobilize them to act to ease suffering. Relevance is great if it offers practical steps and awareness of the world. But the relentless pursuit of it can cause subtle but significant problems. Let me name three.

Collapsing the Distance

In our quest to sound relevant to our listeners, sometimes we let context take the driver's seat. We quickly equate biblical struggles and dramas with what is happening today. We close the gap prematurely or fail to acknowledge that there is one at all. We give insufficient time to our description of the past, making a mad dash to grab its relevance for ourselves. This failure to learn about, honor, and describe ancient Near Eastern cultures well communicates to our listeners that cultural appropriation is acceptable and the lives of the faithful in Scripture were mere backdrops.

We collapse the distance when we fail to honor the past and draw connections in cheap, clever, and superficial ways. Some of us preachers will confess that we know how pleasingly those connections roll off our tongues and how satisfying the smiles or *Amens* are that come at these moments. For example, in the first quarter of the 2020 pandemic, preachers began to announce that "Jeremiah was in quarantine when he was confined to the courtyard." "Paul was in quarantine as the book of Romans ended." "Jonah was under lockdown inside the whale." At first, we liked the clever resonances preachers found with our situation. But, after a while, those parallels added little real value or insight. Some were far-fetched, in a desperate grab for relevance. What worked better were the psalms of lament bravely preached, where preachers skillfully resonated with the psalmist's emotions and let those psalms give voice to our unexpressed pain and fears.

Endless To-Do Lists

Some of us crave a rigorous to-do list. I am solidly in that camp, and yes, I have written down tasks almost completed just so that I could cross them off. Unfortunately, churches pastored by the likes of me can shrink the life of faith to a list-making—and list-completing—endeavor. Every sermon ends with a little list of tasks, making the gospel tragically small. We sense a demand for a to-do list from listeners who view life as a puzzle to complete, a problem to solve, or a program to execute with excellence and diligence. The truth is most of us crave control. We long to believe that life will go well, and evil will stay far from our tent if we tick the right boxes of obedience. This project casts us as the heroes of our own stories, and it reduces the gospel to a set of pragmatic solutions to what ails us. Discipleship quickly deteriorates into frantic doing and earning, and we lose sight of radical grace. We preach to show how God and the gospel of Jesus Christ meet the day's felt need or bothersome problem, usually as it is framed through very Western lenses.

A Fast Fashion Mentality

The fashion industry has an undercurrent called fast fashion. In this stream, clothes are intentionally made very cheaply—they are designed to be worn only a few times and then discarded so that wearers can move on to the next hot look. This trend is troubling for many reasons, including its effects on the environment and fostering of sweatshops and other low-paid labor.[8] But it is also destructive to consumers, who step on that hamster wheel and cannot get off. They are driven by an obsession with the latest, flashiest, shiniest gadgets. This pursuit is a quest for relevance on steroids. Some congregational cultures expect their pastor to insert a witty weekly barb about a misstep made by a political leader on the other side of the aisle from the bulk of the congregation. The tail quickly wags the dog as the quest for "relevant" commentary grabs a preacher's attention more than the more challenging task of carefully and prayerfully studying a Scripture text.

Bearing these cautions about the pursuit of relevance in mind and acknowledging its usefulness as it calls us to the concrete and practical as we preach in the present tense, let's close with one last question for strengthening our pastoral practice of discernment.

Conclusion: (I Wonder) What Should We Always Do?

This question seems too obvious to miss, and yet we do miss it. It is a question that calls us back to our core beliefs and faithful obedience in turbulent times. Sometimes we wring our hands about how to respond to a current event as if it demanded an utterly unique response or a never-before-heard perspective. That is reactive leadership. It yields anxiety and shallow thinking. Responsive leadership anchors us in our foundational truths. It sets us free from the need to dazzle or the ridiculous quest for retweets and likes. Sometimes the timeliest word we can offer is the timeless word. We encourage our people to continue serving and giving as they have been and keep walking the challenging yet life-giving path they have walked. We promise them that our God sees and knows and loves and never changes.

Ask This

- Am I too quick to pronounce regarding current events in my public communication or social media posts or too reluctant?
- What is the pressure I feel from my congregation in this area? How does that shape and limit my ability to speak and lead us towards wise discernment?

---

8. https://sustainablesquare.com/impact-of-fast-fashion.

Try This

- Bring to congregation-wide awareness a directional issue that the leadership is puzzling over. Frame it as a process of ongoing discernment rather than an announcement of a settled decision. Name the competing values and invite the congregation to prayer and thoughtful engagement in a virtual or in-person listening session. (Be sure to get the agreement of your leadership team before doing this.)
- If you are new to naming the work of the Enemy in a given season, be bold this week to articulate what you perceive to be the temptations and threats to the vitality of your community.

7

Preacher as Visionary Prophet
Walking into the Future with Hope

> "Leadership is energizing a community of people toward their own transformation in order to accomplish a shared mission in the face of a changing world."
>
> —TOD BOLSINGER

THE PANDEMIC RAN A wrecking ball through the human capacity to hope. The first casualty in its wake was happiness, as we reluctantly kissed goodbye to countless everyday events that had brought us joy. Whether in classrooms or workspaces, we gave up gathering. We canceled events as simple as a picnic or as crucial as graduation. As it dragged on, the subsequent loss was hope. At its most basic, hope is the capacity to imagine a better future and then move towards it. Of course, it has a deeper theological meaning, but we'll start there. We pride ourselves on our ability to posit a plan, map out the steps, and then walk towards its realization with reasonable confidence. But that capability is not only a point of pride; it is key to our survival. We count on it for organizational growth and stability, and personal sanity. We downgraded every plan to a tentative possibility in the pandemic since everything was in flux. I officiated a wedding in the fall of 2020 that tumbled its way through three different venues, each less attractive than the one before, each guest list shrunk significantly. By the end, even I did not make the cut. Nevertheless, I donned my robe, preached, and pronounced them husband and wife from my kitchen counter via Zoom. The couples' humor and resilience inspired me.

We all have pivoted ourselves dizzy, not to the point of physical nausea but an unsettledness at our core. Solomon spoke poignantly of an aching sickness of heart that overtakes us when our hopes are crushed or delayed (Prov 13:12). As we strive to preach to connect to listeners' hearts in the aftermath of the pandemic, one of our most complicated challenges will be helping listeners access and rearticulate their deepest hopes, which are buried under a pile of disappointments. Some they lost sight of; others they quite deliberately shelved in an emotional triage operation.

This chapter will consider the nature of hope and how we preach to catalyze it. Preaching hope enlists the future tense, articulating what could happen and will happen to reanimate the imagination. It ventures out into a valley full of bones, roots around in the wreckage, and then dares to claim that these bones will live. Bold words of God's future redemptive work awaken our hope, just as preaching God's work in the past fuels our faith.

The Nature of Hope

We will consider hope's paradoxical portrayal in Scripture as both a hefty weight and lifter of our spirits, an indispensable companion on our journey. We'll see how both the need to hope and the act of hoping are part of what makes us human—at once humble and great-hearted—and how the capacity to hope is crucial to discipleship. Then we'll discuss how preaching can awaken and deepen the hope for eternity—and the coming week—in individual listeners and congregations. We find surprising answers as we turn to the Scriptures asking what hope looks like and how it feels.

Hope is Heavy

The weightiness of hope is counterintuitive. We think of hope as giving us wings, making us light-hearted and agile, brightening our spirits, and letting them soar. We resonate more easily with Emily Dickenson's lovely assertion that "Hope is the thing with feathers."[1] Indeed, on many days, it is. But on other days, hope's somber and substantial side shows its face. To our dismay, hope reveals itself to be, *by design*, a burden, like a cumbersome

1. Dickinson, "Hope is the Thing with Feathers," poem 254, *Complete Poems*.

brick in our backpack. The images of hope in the New Testament are not feathers but heavy items like helmets (1 Thess 5:8) and anchors (Heb 6:19). How is *that* encouraging news?

In Scripture, weightier was usually better. Glory has weight; chaff does not. Hope is substantial; it is a hassle to carry and utterly indispensable to bring along. But an inert brick is far too flat an image since Scripture portrays hope as agile and alive (1 Pet 1:3). Let's imagine hope as an uninvited traveling companion. She doesn't say much but instead does something strange—she places her firm hand on our back as we walk. At first, this touch might be unwelcome, until we realize that the path ahead is treacherous and her steadying hand is propelling us forward.

Let's take a closer look at the striking image the writer of Hebrews uses to convey hope's heaviness, the anchor for the soul (Heb 6:19). A ship's anchor is indispensable, yet at the beginning of a journey, its sheer weight can feel like an impediment to getting underway. We are sorely tempted to cut the rope and send it sliding overboard. Many of our church communities feel this temptation today. We think, "If we jettison our most outrageous hopes, the journey will be easier to execute." And it is, at least at first. We can tack more quickly. But when we look more closely at this odd image in Hebrews, the anchor is not there to encumber our boat—indeed, it seems not even to be on our boat at all. Instead, it has leaped ahead of us into the holy place, from which it is functioning more like a powerful lure, tethering us to and pulling us toward the very presence of God.[2] "We have this hope, a sure and steadfast anchor of the soul, a hope that enters the inner shrine behind the curtain, where Jesus . . . has entered." Hope here is not burdening us but rather is a mighty magnet drawing us into the presence of God.

That is a beautiful vision. And yet, in our everyday pastoral work, as we listen to people who have endured profound disappointments, from the loss of parents or a child to the abrupt end of a career, it can feel almost cruel to ask them to continue to hope. It is heartless if we do so without naming the losses and sorrow with empathy. We must acknowledge that continuing to hope after disappointment renders us vulnerable to more disappointment.

In the wake of a crisis, church leaders themselves might find themselves thinking, "Let's stop dreaming crazy dreams for how God could work in our city through our church. After what we have all been through, it will

---

2. It is unclear where the boat is in the metaphor in Hebrews 6:19. Some scholars understand the anchor as more like a docking system or a pulley.

be more realistic to focus on a high-quality Sunday service and a balanced budget. Let's keep our dreams small and manageable." As individuals and families, we do the same and seek the vision that will carry the least risk of disappointment. Untethered from and unburdened by our initial, more ambitious vision, we do make swifter progress. But what we tend to discover is that after going a little way down that road, we hit a dead end. We then return to the starting point and realize that we must walk the arduous road of radical hope to live as faithful disciples. Hope insists on staying by our side, the companion whose strong hand at our back steadies, orients, and guides us. That picture roots hope in a relationship with God, who is the source and the ultimate destination of our hope. Indeed, God promises to *be* our hope (Joel 3:16).

Hope Lifts and Changes Us

When we reckon honestly with the heaviness of hope, it can sound like the traveling companion we would love to ditch at the next train station. Yet, hope does not let us so quickly abandon it. Instead, it insists on accompanying us, fortunately for us. We will fail to arrive without it. As we take on the weight of hope, we discover this wonderful paradox, that hope also lifts us. Hope enables us to rise above our hardships.

How does hope invigorate us for the journey? First, it begins to free us from anxiety, which is a purely destructive weight. As we receive hope, we find that we can relax and travel lightheartedly, enjoying the unfolding story because we know the ending, at least in part. Second, it awakens us. Because we believe in a God who reliably meets us in our distress with help and gracious presence, we stand on the lookout for the shape that rescue will take this time. We cultivate curiosity. Finally, hope invites us to travel differently, living more vulnerably towards others. As Lischer puts it, "[W]ith hope in your heart, your ethics change. For hope is a way of living openly and generously toward others."[3]

This traveling companion named hope is a born teacher. She teaches us to wait patiently and suffer faithfully. We see in Scripture that people of hope can endure great hardship, and surprisingly, their hope even *grows* in that soil. Lischer says, "Hope thrives in its natural habitat, which is distress."[4] Faith in God engenders hope. We see this happen for Joseph in

---

3. Lischer, *Just Tell the Truth*, 55.
4. Lischer, *Just Tell the Truth*, 54.

prison and the band of disciples praising God during the persecution in the book of Acts. They could have chosen to turn inward in bitterness or away from God in resentment. By choosing hope, they allowed God's story to unfold within and through them. Hope shapes the church into a resilient band of sojourners. As theologian Rowan Williams observed, "[T]he church needs to be marked by profound patience: patience with actual humans in their confusions and uncertainties . . . patience in that we realize it takes time for each one of us to grow up into Christ. Hope and patience belong together. Only a church that is learning patience can proclaim hope effectively."[5] I would add that preachers must learn patience to proclaim anything well.

Hope Makes Us Human

If the pandemic stunted our capacity to hope, it also struck a blow to the core of what makes us human. But if we lean into the gifts of this challenging season, we may find that it has been deepening our capacity to carry true hope, even as it has increased our neediness. The human experience compels us to live with unfulfilled desires, which ideally cause us to turn to God. We are needy and incomplete, created to live in humble and glad dependence on our Creator. We have had ample opportunity to practice being creatures lately.

The very act of hoping humbles us. Our longing for more spurs us to articulate what we have not yet attained. We confess our finitude and our lack. That practice positions us to hope. Augustine wrote, "Only to the humble is it given to hope."[6] To hope is to admit that we receive our future; we do not fashion it ourselves. We cannot bring about that for which we hope, at least not if we are hoping as boldly as God created us to, longing for nothing less than new heavens and new earth and crying, "Come, Lord Jesus."

Theologian Emmanuel Katangole urges us to humility born of gratitude when he writes, "The church herself is the story of hope, constituted through the death and resurrection of Christ. This [points to] the unique tonality of Christian hope, which must avoid any traits of triumphalism, but must preserve the elements of gift, gratitude, and surprise at the heart

---

5. Williams, *Being Disciples*, 30.
6. Augustine, *Expositions of the Psalms*, Psalm 118.

of a Christian experience of hope."[7] Preaching in the future tense lays bare the gap between what is and what will be and reminds listeners to embrace humility because they know they have not yet arrived.

While hope both grows humility and requires humility, the happy irony is that while we are confessing our smallness before God, the act of hoping *enlarges* us. Aquinas developed the striking concept of the "great-hearted" person, one who possesses a *magnus animus* (a great soul or spirit), from which we get our word *magnanimity*. In our casual use of the term, we flatten and shrink its meaning down to the capacity to forgive a minor debt. "Fortunately, the ticket collector was feeling magnanimous today."

Aquinas had much more in mind. The quality of magnanimity was central to his understanding of the life of discipleship. He conceived life as a pilgrimage that required a great-hearted spirit to take the first step and every subsequent one. He called it an arduous but possible journey. Both descriptors are crucial. Aquinas urged followers of Jesus to embrace the demanding nature of the journey but take heart that the journey is possible—it *will* end well with the help of God. Not only will the journey end well, but *we* will end well; the journey will change us for the better. As Aquinas scholar Josef Pieper puts it, "A person is magnanimous if he has the courage to seek what is great and become worthy of it."[8]

Magnanimity grows within us through a lively process Aquinas described as the *extensio animi ad magna*[9]—stretching the spirit towards what is excellent. In this case, the endpoint we strain towards is being at home with God. There is an innocence in Aquinas's picture of hopeful and magnanimous pilgrims, who possess childlike willingness to stretch their spirits toward God, look foolish, and dream big. Pieper comments on Aquinas's portrayal of magnanimous hope within the youthful pilgrim. He writes, "It alone can [make people] at once relaxed and disciplined, with adaptability and readiness, that strong-hearted freshness, that resilient joy, that steady perseverance in trust that so distinguish the young and makes them loveable."[10]

Magnanimity makes us courageous, joyful, and willing to risk boldly. Aquinas described this arduous yet joyful pilgrimage as one that only the greathearted begin and the humble complete. Magnanimity and humility

---

7. Katangole, *Born from Lament*, 33–34.
8. Pieper, *Faith, Hope, and Love*, 101.
9. Aquinas, cited in Pieper, *Faith, Hope, and Love*, 101.
10. Pieper, *Faith, Hope, and Love*, 111.

work together to keep us on the path. Hope-infused humility keeps us from falling into presumption, the arrogant false belief that we have already arrived and attained our goal. Presumption robs us of what he calls the *status viatoris*, the mindset of a traveler. But an equal danger lurks. Without magnanimity born of hope, we fall into despair, the false belief that we will never arrive. For an entirely different reason, we also lose the pilgrim mindset in despair. Presumption puts our car in park because we arrogantly assume we are already where we need to be. Despair catches us in its nets and paralyzes us.

As you preach to a post-pandemic world, where "getting back to normal" is top on listeners' minds, how will you craft sermons that not only tap specific hopes but, more importantly, form hopeful people? How will you cultivate your listeners' *status viatoris*, their pilgrim mindset? How will you awaken a love for the journey, a passionate desire for the journey's end, and a humble yet capacious heart as we travel? That vocation is *your* arduous journey, perhaps now more than ever.

Preaching Our Ultimate Hope

As we invite others to walk the road of discipleship with hope, they will need hearty sustenance. Like Elijah, who heard, "Eat and drink or the journey will be too much for you" (1 Kgs 19:7), we need nourishment so we will be strong enough to carry hope as we travel. Fortunately, preaching is up to the task. As Luke Powery put it, "Preaching midwifes hope into the world, and when it is born, it will not disappoint."[11] If preaching is not on some level fueling hope, it has departed from its core task. Let us consider how we declare God's future to instill hope. We will first discuss why we need to regularly preach our *ultimate* hope, then why and how we preach vision for next week and next year.

Preaching the eschaton, the end of history as we know it now, is complicated. Some of us are reeling from hearing it done poorly, with complex timelines matching disturbing prophetic imagery with current international events and political leaders. In a bid to avoid that, we omit it altogether. We figure that narrating the past and discerning the present is challenging enough. Foretelling the future takes that difficulty and uncertainty to a new level, so it scares some of us away altogether.

---

11. Powery, *Dem Dry Bones*, 50.

But if we take our preaching cues from Scripture, we notice that its leaders regularly and confidently announced a reality they could not yet see. They did so because preaching God's future is an act of leadership. It is a crucial tool as we seek to energize congregations toward the transformation Bolsinger spoke of above. As Eugene Peterson put it, "Without eschatology, the line goes slack, and nothing is pulling us to the heights, to holiness, to the prize of the high calling in Christ Jesus."[12]

Preaching about God's future involves the bold proclamation of four themes, all of which have Jesus Christ solidly at their center. First, he is coming again. The Advent season invites us to preach at least once each year on the second coming of Christ, but ideally, we should voice our longing for that day more often. His arrival will bring us the joy of being in his presence. We long to see God's face, to be united with God. Preaching about the future should tap that longing. Christ's presence will usher in our redemption, healing, and restoration, as shame and guilt are wiped away. "All now mysterious shall be bright at last."[13]

As we look out on the far horizon in hope-filled watching and waiting, we find that the path in front of us is more straightforward. We can better glimpse the grace that is all around us right now. When we preach God's ultimate future, we equip our listeners with courage and hope to face the sometimes frightening intermediate future.

Second, we preach that those who have died in Christ will be resurrected bodily. Our physical resurrection by Christ's power is a powerful theme as we struggle on earth with our exceedingly vulnerable bodies—as the pandemic constantly reminded us.

Third, the future will involve judgment, which sounds sobering at best and possibly even frightening. But it is radically encouraging news. It means God will set things right and hold evildoers accountable. That gives us peace and renders us peacemakers. We can let God settle scores. We can know that God will mercifully yet painstakingly purify us. Our confident expectation of the coming judgment of God clears the path for healing.

Fourth, creation will undergo a great restoration, renewal, and redemption. As Wright puts it, "The hope is that God will eventually do for the whole creation what he did for Jesus; God is at work in the present, by

---

12. Peterson, *Under the Unpredictable Plant*, 144.
13. From the hymn "Be Still My Soul."

the Spirit of Jesus, to prepare the world for that great remaking, that great unveiling of the future plan."[14]

Given the potency of these four themes, it is tragic that we so often neglect to preach our hope of God's coming kingdom. As Long notes, "True gospel proclamation is always thoroughgoingly eschatological. [It] is not only a word about God's future, but it is also a word from God's future that interrupts and disrupts the expectations of the present tense with the crisis of God's advent."[15] Jürgen Moltmann agrees. "From first to last, and not merely in the epilogue, Christianity is eschatology, is hope, forward-looking and forward moving, and therefore also revolutionizing and transforming the present. The eschatological is not one element of Christianity, but it is the medium of Christian faith as such, the key in which everything in it is set, the glow that suffuses everything here in the dawn of an expected new day."[16]

God's promised future is bright and joyful, and so we pursue the challenging task of inviting even those who wait in sorrow to rejoice in at least a corner of their hearts as they do so. Preaching about God's future will form a powerful antidote to despair and discouragement. It will energize us and kindle our desire for prayer and worship, and it will also change how we relate to others. The future God is bringing intends to shape our practices and patterns today. Therefore, preaching about the future should compel us to hasten it, to welcome it, and to act in ways that mirror the pictures of it we see in Scripture. The end comes to us as a gracious gift; we are not primarily bringing it to pass. But we do get to participate in it as we foster vibrant faith communities and live as agents of grace in our neighborhoods and homes. For this reason, we not only preach our eternal hopes, but we also lead our people by articulating a bold vision for the season—and the week—just ahead of us.

Preaching Vision for Next Month and the Decade Ahead

If you have ever been part of a team or an organization at an inflection point and heard its leader passionately articulate a vision for growth—insightfully naming the costs and rallying stakeholders to pay them—you know how motivating that can be. Even if you've only seen it in a movie,

---

14. https://ntwrightpage.com/2016/04/04/apocalypse-now/.
15. Long, "Preaching God's Future," 195.
16. Moltmann, *Theology of Hope*, 16.

you know that such moments are defining. They are catalytic for organizations and individuals, whether employees, beleaguered athletic teams, or bands of outnumbered warriors. Visionary leaders make us want to join the team as it suits up to realize a dream, and they make us willing to sacrifice alongside the team. Bold and big plans always cost us, and they change us as we pay that cost. As a result, our enthusiasm grows, and our commitment deepens.

Since the reality is that secular leaders (and fictional characters in movies) are often better at this than many of us who lead churches, we should learn all we can from the speeches of sports coaches, CEOs, and change agents in our culture. How do they win trust? How do they build urgency and elicit desire? How do they overcome fear and inertia as they call people to action? It is valuable to study their strategies, but we do so with the awareness that the source of our authority and the grounds for our hope are often fundamentally different. The grounds for their hope are entirely human effort, and they lack a vision of a Creator graciously giving us a promising future we do not earn or deserve. Most of these speeches are rooted in optimistic confidence in the power of "progress." Wright reminds us, "Hope has to do, not with steady progress, but with the belief that the world is God's world, and that God has continuing plans for it."[17]

We are hungry for reliable mapping apps that will calmly direct us towards the desired future in seasons of sustained chaos, assuring us we are making steady progress. But turn-by-turn directions for church and individual thriving in Christ are no longer available if they ever were. Nor are they what we most need. Instead of itineraries, what the Scriptures excel at are poetic visions. The prophets used poetry to paint dramatic pictures of graveyards full of bones coming back to life. So did Jesus, with his banquets and feasts, and Peter, with his portrait of the church as a living temple. From Isaiah to Revelation, gorgeous images of the future interrupt our present and declare that it could be different, even now. When we read of the diverse multitude standing and singing praise before the throne and the Lamb, this motivates us to see if our worship here on earth could more closely approximate that diverse and yet united celebration.

So let your language be lavish and even poetic. Try your hand at a metaphor. Take a risk with alliteration or with repetition of a striking phrase. The prophets invoked the language of poetry to enlarge the imaginations of people whose vision had shrunk down to the survival and maintenance

---

17. https://ntwrightpage.com/2016/04/04/apocalypse-now/.

tasks in front of their noses. Their lovely and lively images infused the atmosphere with fresh hope, energizing dejected people to live more wholeheartedly in the present. For some preachers, that does not come naturally. It grows in part by reading the poetic passages of Scripture and by reading other poets and simply trying it out—daring to flesh out a concept with a vivid image. As we develop the skill of preaching the future, let's consider six key features that will mark visionary preaching.

1. Visionary Preaching Creates Space for Lament

A visionary sermon often begins with a lament. Ugandan theologian Emmanuel Katangole reflects profoundly on the suffering of his nation and continent. He sees lament as the starting point of hope. He describes the practice of lament as a "form of turning to God in the midst of the ruins."[18] It sometimes involves a brutally honest naming of current reality, which may evoke anger, deep disappointment, grief, and regret. When we set out to preach a sermon that gives listeners a godly vision for how their church could better serve its neighborhood, we may need to begin by confessing the current reality of our church's distance from our neighbors and their needs.

Our sermons may begin with a bright, joyful picture such as that of the body of Christ in Ephesians 3 or the joyfully worshiping nations in Revelation 7. However, honest, visionary sermons will eventually work their way to lament with a sentence like this one: "Let's face it; this is not where we are today." The gap that we papered over has been exposed. Everyone sees it, so we may as well talk about it. In the clear light of beautiful biblical visions, we see the ugly division and brokenness in our land even more clearly. This clarity leads us to lament, grieve, and cry out to God for change.

Far from allowing us to escape into idle daydreams of the future, biblical visions sharpened the contrast between the hoped-for and the current reality. The act of praying, "May your kingdom come on earth as it is in heaven," provokes us to ask, "Why is earth so unlike heaven?" "Why are our efforts at creation care so anemic?" "Why has it proven so challenging to fully integrate our churches in ways that express fierce solidarity, justice, and love?" Even in Scripture's most hopeful visions, lament lurks not far off to the side. For example, in Revelation 22, God provides a tree whose leaves possess the power to heal the nations—an implicit acknowledgment that

---

18. Katangole, *Born from Lament*, 25.

those ethnic groups are in deep need of healing. Naming current pain in our sermons is crucial to the integrity of visionary preaching.

It also builds our credibility. We trust leaders when we believe they see reality.

Listeners in our churches will react to hyped-up, pipe-dream visions with skepticism or outright cynicism. They have been fooled before; their hopes have been dashed one too many times. Previous church communities proved more toxic and life-draining than the vibrant photos on their website made them seem. They will not trust you to articulate a vision unless they know that you see the present, empathize with its pain, and assess the risks. A credible leader is clear-eyed about the hardship required to reach the desired destination and promises to walk with them every step of the way there. Lament prepares a leader to do that.

2. *Visionary Preaching Comforts Us and Helps Us to Endure*

The people who first heard John's letter of Revelation were struggling. The churches of Asia lived under the boot of the Roman Empire. They had endured the cruel persecution of Nero in the previous generation, and the emperor Domitian had not backed off. They may have been lamenting the destruction of Jerusalem itself, or they could see that it was coming soon. It would have breathed so much courage into their weary hearts to hear, "Life lived fully in God's presence, with every tear wiped away, with every ethnic group bringing its gifts—this is your bright and certain future." God gave John extravagant pictures of heavenly realities to encourage the churches enduring hardship on earth. Visionary preaching vividly describes a reality that will come to pass for a people whose hope is wavering. That encourages hearers to persevere when the journey is long and hard. As Jordan Peterson puts it, "A vision of the desirable future . . . links action taken now with important, long-term, foundational values. It lends actions in the present significance and importance. It provides a frame limiting uncertainty and anxiety."[19]

---

19. Peterson, *12 Rules for Life*, 213.

3. Visions Shape Priorities

I lived for many years in a valley with steep mountains to the north of town. I'm not great with directions, but I never struggled with east or west while I lived there. The mountains reliably oriented me. Biblical visions, including those we preach, are those mountains. They tell us where we are headed. That clear orientation can guide discernment processes when we are embroiled in conflict over strategic priorities for our budget and staffing. For example, if your church were to craft a vision that three years from now, you hoped to be an intentionally multiethnic church in every aspect of your worship and life together, that vision would shape priorities and guide planning. "Therefore, here is what we'll be doing more of, and here is what we'll be doing less." You'll notice in that sentence that there may be a perception of winners and losers among the stakeholders who hear that. "What? Fewer potlucks? That's my favorite part of church." Every vision involves losses and costs. Every vision sermon should include a sentence like, "This is what it will cost." But we will quickly follow that with, "Here is the joyful opportunity. This is what that sacrifice will make space for."

Visions often come into play at a point of crisis or at least directional change for an organization or a nation, which are usually moments of heightened anxiety. A vision spoken into that moment gives the gift of peace and clarity to hearers.

4. Visions Unite Us

Big and inclusive visions for our communities of faith invite us to transcend our differences to achieve them. We all leave agreeing, "Whatever else divides us, we can come together around this." Of course, visions do not always unite, and many political or theological talks come with the explicit intention of separating people into camps. When a vision is rooted in a leader's grandiose dreams, it inevitably divides people. It is a mark of humility to preach a generous sermon that honors the differences in our midst and plumbs deep enough to find common ground. Inclusive visions let many people gather around them, offering multiple entry points and handles to grasp.

When we seek to unite a community, one of our best tools is a hopeful story. We've discussed the power of stories in chapter 5, but here we also note their ability to unite us. As we listen, we grow in our shared hunger to live like the characters in a story. Such stories awaken our imagination for what could be. Katangole writes,

> [Stories] display the concrete, practical, and lived reality of that hope. In this respect, hope is essentially different from optimism, in that more than being a stated hope, it is a narrated hope. To use the language of 1 Peter 1:3, it is a *living* hope. The church herself *is* the story of hope, constituted through the death and resurrection of Christ. This [points to] the unique tonality of Christian hope, which must avoid any traits of triumphalism but must preserve the elements of gift, gratitude, and surprise at the heart of a Christian experience of hope.[20]

5. Visions Turn Us to Prayer

The beauty of a vision we receive from God is that it is not ultimately our job, nor in our power, to make it come to pass. Visions are not blueprints to implement or a commander's marching orders. Jesus did not say to us, "Here is what my kingdom should look like; now you get out there and hustle with all of your might to build it." Instead, he painted pictures that drew us towards it with delight and then promised that God would gladly give it to us (Luke 12:32). God does not ask us to create the kingdom—God brings it, though he invites us to participate in it and to live in ways that point to it and give delicious foretastes of it. The picture John saw was a city *coming down* as a gift.

If we build God's kingdom with our tools, tactics, and strength, we are prone to both anxiety and pride. But if we are receiving it, we position ourselves to catch it well, with patience and eager hope, in glad dependence on our Creator.

6. Visions Call Us to Specific Actions

Striking images and inspiring stories are essential to the power of visionary speech. But since you hope your preaching will inspire concrete action, you will want the sermon to reach a point of tight specificity, sharpening your topic down to one clear and memorable sentence or phrase, which you may repeat a few times. For example, visionary sermons will include sentences like, "Here is one step each of us could take this week," "This is one change

---

20. Katangole, *Born from Lament*, 33–34.

our leadership team is making this month," or, "This is one way we could welcome newcomers better next week."

One of the specific actions we need to call members to is generous giving. Many of us are more comfortable asking for people's time than their money. But the reality is that successful ministry leaders ask people to give their treasure, time, and talent. When we do this, we help people align their hearts with their treasure (Matt 6:21). We help them grow in generosity. It is exciting to watch a faith community begin to live out of a culture of abundance instead of scarcity and to see them give their resources to what matters. If we genuinely believe that the mission of our church is worthy of investment, we will be glad to invite others to invest.

Conclusion

True, biblical hope is agile and robust because it does not cling to cherished scenarios, making them the measure of whether our hopes came to pass. My friends who got married on Zoom could respond with grace and resilience to the relentless pivoting away from the wedding of their dreams because their ultimate hope was to *be married*, not to pull off a dream wedding. If they had pinned their hopes on that, the months leading up to it would have been miserable. Instead, it was a season of improbable contentment and peace. Hope is, at times, a hefty weight to carry—it requires endurance and faithfulness. But hope is alive and lightens our spirits even as we carry it, whereas expectations and demands upon the future are only dead weight. Let them go. When we detach ourselves from grasping for specific outcomes, we find something remarkable has happened. We are free—both lighthearted and greathearted, able to receive, embrace, and enjoy what comes.

To review our tour of verb tenses, the core task of preaching the *past* is lively storytelling. The fruit of listening well to the past is faith formation, the nurture of a story-formed people steeped in the biblical world's values. The central task of preaching the *present* is discernment, and the fruit it bears is a community of people wise to the movements of the Spirit in their midst, and therefore ready to love boldly. Finally, the crucial task of preaching the *future* is imparting hope, which fuels radical discipleship. We have made our way to what endures, according to Paul in 1 Corinthians 13:13— faith, hope, and love. The greatest is love, lived out in the present. But love is strengthened as we look back on the past with gratitude that fuels faith, and we look ahead to the future with joyful hope.

Ask This:

- Take some time to reflect on what the struggles of this past season have cost you in terms of hopefulness. Ask the Lord to renew hope within you where it has waned.
- With your leadership team, assess where your faith community is marked by hopefulness and where it is struggling to hope. How could you strengthen your verbal leadership so that it more effectively catalyzed hope within your members?

Try This:

- If you excel at lavish descriptions of bright futures and are less clear on specific actions, work hard to craft a few well-defined steps listeners could take in the week and month following your next few sermons. Root those steps in the gracious initiative of God so they avoid the feel of a to-do list.
- If the opposite is true, challenge yourself to be more poetic as you help listeners envision the good future God is bringing. Soak in Isaiah 50–65 and other prophetic visions and learn from them.

8

Preacher as Leader

Choosing and Using Modes of Influence

"[Leadership] lies not only in recognizing that not all human influences are coercive and exploitative, and that not all transactions among persons are mechanical, transactional, and ephemeral. It lies in seeing that the most powerful influences consist of deeply human relationships in which two or more persons *engage* with one another."

—JAMES MACGREGOR BURNS

PREACHING IS FUNDAMENTALLY AN act of leadership. We are in this to influence. Some of us hear that and say, "Sign me up!" We are entirely comfortable not only influencing but even commanding. Given the choice of seat in a racing boat, we seek out the role of coxswain precisely so we can shout orders the whole length of the race. Others of us love the caring and teaching dimensions of pastoral work but find that exerting influence does not come naturally at all. We must fortify ourselves with multiple internal pep talks before entering settings requiring us to be in command. Even in meetings where we are given the reins and asked to provide direction, we punt to asking thoughtful questions, exploring alternatives, expressing empathy—anything but telling others what to do. This chapter will help you assess your sermons for their use of speech that influences and persuades listeners to act. That examination may reveal uncomfortable or encouraging things about you as a leader. Some of us need more backbone and courage; some of us are sorely lacking in gentleness and patience.

Hopefully, as pastors, we are never directly commanding in a drill sergeant's mode. But we sought a leadership role partly because we are not satisfied with organizations as they are. We hunger for our faith communities to experience more joyful transformation as they live in response to the leadership of God. We long to see them freshly energized to grow and serve together. Since we understand that preaching is one of the critical levers of influence available to us, we need to ask, "What tools of influence in spoken communication spark change within listeners? Which ones am I overusing, and which am I neglecting?"

This chapter answers those questions through the lens of what grammar nerds call the *modes* of a verb, the indicative, imperative, and subjunctive. Each mode influences differently. Verbs in the unassuming indicative mode simply make statements that define or describe reality. This book has already discussed several common uses of the indicative without calling attention to mode. When we testify, teach wisdom, and declare the truth about God and his work in the past, present, and future, we usually speak in the indicative. Consider these three indicative-mode sentences:

"The sky is dense with angry dark clouds."

"This cake is so delicious!"

"The Lord is unwaveringly faithful."

At first glance, these utterances seem to bring little or no intention to influence. How could stating them be an act of leadership? However, if you were listening and debating whether to bring an umbrella, pick up a dessert fork, or head out in a risky missional venture—and you trusted the speaker—the assertions above would guide you, wouldn't they? They would compel you to act differently in response to hearing them. The humble indicative packs a bigger punch than it seems to at first glance. Often in Scripture, sentences phrased in the indicative prepare the ground for more explicit calls to change in the imperative or subjunctive modes.

The imperative is the form we use for commands. Paul often builds a foundation with truths about the beauty of God just before issuing a command. For example, "The Lord is at hand; *do not be anxious* about anything" (Phil 4:5). The subjunctive mode's use is more subtle and varied; we'll unpack that shortly. It is an overlooked tool in preaching that allows us to lead by imagining, encouraging, and inviting. We need to learn to use both the imperative and subjunctive modes with confidence in our sermons. Yet, it is striking how often in Scripture speakers trust the indicative to do the job of influencing all on its own. Let's begin with that mode and then consider how to use the imperative and the subjunctive modes with skill and grace.

Using the Indicative Well

Verbs spoken in the indicative mode simply assert or describe. That makes them sound flat and lifeless compared to the mighty imperative. But make no mistake, compelling descriptions *do* things. If we listen well to them, they can change us. Vivid descriptions of the beauty of creation invite us to cherish it, give thanks to its Creator, and work for its preservation and flourishing. Likewise, a faithful rendering of the beauty of Jesus Christ invites us to trust in and worship him. Here we will look at how indicative speech excels at three preaching tasks: highlighting what we could miss, honoring people and acts, and reframing problems.

Highlighting

Sometimes a brief articulation of truth can knock us off our feet. I heard one of those in an emergency room a few years ago. My sister Ruth excelled at noticing, whether it was my new nail polish color ("Ooh, sis, that is *so* pretty!") or that the macaroni and cheese was the yummiest she'd ever had. With her cognitive impairment from a congenital disability, her words were always simple, yet at times surprisingly profound. She watched carefully, even in the hardest of times. One evening in her final week, I sat by her gurney in an emergency room as Ruth worked hard for every breath. Her stomach was huge and tight as a drum due to a blocked intestine. Tubes were everywhere. She had just rated her pain level a ten out of ten. Kathy, the ER nurse, had left after kindly doing what little she could to make her comfortable.

I could tell Ruth wanted to say something, so I leaned in close, guessing she would ask for more ice chips or another pillow. Instead, with immense effort yet also with satisfied contentment, she slowly eked out, "Oh, sis, Kathy is a *really* great nurse, don't you think?" I caught my breath to hear that it was this thought that sprang to her mind rather than a complaint about the myriad tubes. I sat in awe of this lovely human, who had taught me so much about living with disabilities as she gave me a master class in how to die. She died noticing what was excellent and beautiful in others.

Ruth preached with power that day. As she highlighted what I had missed, she did not need to fortify her splendid words with a command or an appeal. I did not need her to say, "*You* should try appreciating people more, sis." It was enough. Simply listening to her words caused a desire to well up within me to live differently, pay better attention to the good around me, and speak about what I see. Evocative description sometimes prepares the way for commands or exhortations. Sometimes it stands alone. My sister made a habit of telling the truth about the kindness she perceived in people. She needed a lot of help with daily living, so she had ample opportunity to see people being compassionate. She regularly noted that with gratitude. Here Ruth held one of the secrets to preaching that describes reality well: she savored what she saw. Ellen Davis calls this the capacity to be astonished. Speaking of our need to let Scripture astonish us, Davis writes,

> I suppose every one of us would like to be an astonishing preacher—unlikely though that seems on a week-to-week basis. But the plain fact is that no preacher can ever be astonishing (in a positive sense!) unless she has first been astonished. And the only regular and fully reliable source of astonishment for the Christian preacher is Scripture itself. Therefore, my aim . . . is to explore the Old Testament as a perpetual source of astonishment and, moreover, to consider how it is that we as preachers can put ourselves in the way of that astonishment, so as to be overtaken by it.[1]

I agree with Davis and add that the Lord also invites us to cultivate astonishment at the beauty of nature and the people around us. We can best employ the indicative to do its work when we attend to Scripture, creation, and the humans for whom we are cultivating affection and then speak aloud what we see. We see God do this when he stops creating each day to behold his work, savor it, and say, "This is good. This is very good." Jesus excelled at attending, noticing, and speaking about the qualities he saw in people, from the faith they displayed as they pursued healing for themselves or their children to the generosity of the widow in the temple or the gratitude of the leper who returned to thank him. He was lavish with his praise of others as they stumbled toward him. And he was tireless in telling the beautiful truth about his Father's gracious ways. As preachers, we need to cultivate our ability to stop long enough to be astonished by life and describe what we see.

1. Davis, *Wondrous Depth*, 2.

Honoring

The indicative mode can work powerfully in the pulpit to *honor* hidden work and faithful saints in our midst. This, too, is leadership. In a church I had recently begun to lead, I noticed a group that regularly sat in the last row of the church and left as soon as the service was over. Their posture and crossed arms displayed their distance and disengagement. I was curious. I learned that they were the team that prepared a monthly dinner for persons experiencing homelessness. I joined them the first Friday I could and then reflected on the importance of their work in my next sermon. My intention was not to flatter them but to honor their work. I also wanted to move it from the margin to the center—to reframe this service opportunity from something already covered by this outlier team, which was the congregation's perception, to a ministry all of us could join. That seemed straightforward and unremarkable to me. But that Sunday, they stayed. They told me ruefully that the previous pastor had said to them that what they did to serve the poor was "not central to the church's mission." No wonder they were estranged! I never could get them to move up from their cherished last pew, but at least they lingered happily after the service from then on.

My words in the pulpit that day were prompted in part by the wise advice of preaching professor Anna Carter Florence, who writes, "We can't preach to people we don't love. We may not always *like* our listeners, but we have to love them. If we don't love them yet, it is up to us to figure out a way to do it; that is our responsibility as preachers. It is up to us to watch them closely, to discover what is beautiful about them, to practice attending and describing so that we see those things and name them."[2]

Reframing

In addition to description's power to highlight and honor, the indicative excels at framing and reframing problems. As it does so, it shifts perceptions and shapes values. This world is confusing and overwhelming, and someone who can offer an interpretive lens so we can understand troubling events will quickly gain a following. Leaders who can help us map our way to meaning and purpose regarding current realities can be powerfully persuasive for good or for harm. They do this by naming our point of pain, articulating its source or cause, and arousing the desire for something better—and possibly inciting fears of a dreaded future. On a global level, Hitler,

---

2. Florence, *Preaching as Testimony*, 153.

Pol Pot, and other dictators defined and framed the overarching problem of their times in ways that resonated with the fears and hopes of listeners. It is reassuring to have the problem framed such that we know with certainty who our enemies are and what will save us.

Good leaders catalyze positive, lasting change by doing descriptive work with truth and integrity. Accurate framing of a problem is an invaluable gift to an organization or an individual in distress. For example, when a congregation accurately perceives its neighborhood's needs, it can move with great energy to alleviate harm and foster human flourishing. Likewise, when we insightfully frame the challenges of our current moment, our members will be more able to flourish within them.

Wise leaders know that their job is not only to comfort and reassure people. Sometimes a more accurate reframing of a problem lets us see that it is far worse than we had perceived, we are more complicit than we had understood, or the pathway to transformation will involve more suffering than we had grasped. For example, Jesus' indicative-mode statements often flipped our conceptions upside down about who was the greatest, what kind of people would inherit the earth, and who would enter the kingdom first. Jesus' metaphors about his Father's kingdom disoriented as much as they delighted. We hear them and think, "Wait a minute! The seating charts for these banquets are all off. And persecution can't *possibly* be a source of blessing." As we absorb the shock of his words, we become compelled to ask, "How are these startling descriptions of reality inviting me to live differently in response?"

Watch how Barbara Brown Taylor reframes our perceived unfairness problem as we hear the parable of the workers in the vineyard lined up to get their pay. For most of the sermon, she nurtures our sympathies with the workers who showed up at the crack of dawn and worked diligently. Then she slyly muses,

> The most curious thing about the parable for me is where we locate ourselves in line. The story sounds quite different from the end of the line than it does from the front of the line, but isn't it interesting that ninety-nine percent of us hear it from the front row seats? We are the ones who have gotten the short end of the stick; we are the ones who have been cheated. We are the ones who have gotten up early and stayed late and worked hard and all for what? That is how most of us hear the parable, but it is entirely possible that we are mistaken about where we are in line. Suppose for a moment that it is you back there. As far as God is concerned,

we are halfway around the block. By starting at the end of the lines, with the last and the least, God lets us know that his ways are not our ways, and that if we want to see things his way, we might question our own notions of what is fair, and why we get so upset when our lines do not work.[3]

Taylor subtly yet insistently "recasts" us in the parable in a way that dramatically reframes our perception of who we are and what it is we need from God. Her sermon challenges me to my core, and yet this paragraph contains only one imperative ("Suppose it is you back there") and one subjunctive (we might question . . ."). Instead, Taylor trusts the power of well-crafted descriptive speech to astonish us as it reframes and to convict us as it recasts us.

Some of us need to trust description to do its work. We feel anxious unless every sermon ends with four practical steps to take. We fail to notice that many potent speech events in Scripture linger on description and then simply end with it. Psalm 23 has indelibly shaped countless lives by doing little more than portraying well what the psalmist grasped about his Shepherd and Lord. Still, some of us preach a purely evocative sermon and feel vaguely guilty that we haven't done our job. Sometimes transformative preaching really is as simple as poet Mary Oliver's instructions for living: "Pay Attention. Be Astonished. Tell about it."[4]

Sometimes, though, we stop at a description when more is needed. We stop there because, in our minds, the implications are obvious. We think the next steps are so clear that they don't need to be spoken in cases when our listeners would benefit from concrete suggestions. When we hear multiple sermons in a row that never leave the indicative, we feel the lack because we know deep down that we humans need more leadership than description alone provides. Some preachers stop there because they enjoy poetic description and engaging teaching so much that they don't want to leave that mode. I had a doctor who loved to teach, usually accompanied by incomprehensible drawings of my innards scribbled on the paper that covered the cold table where I perched. I appreciated his desire to educate me, but by the end, I grew antsy to hear not just elaborate diagnoses but a prescription and an action plan. That is what the imperative does best.

---

3. Taylor, "Beginning at the End," 19 (edited for brevity).
4. Oliver, "Sometimes," 104.

Using the Imperative Well

If the indicative lets us savor creation and Creator—as we might while strolling a country lane with a wide-eyed child, savoring together a dragonfly's luminescent wings—the imperative is the mode we shift to when that child has dashed into a busy street at the end of the lane. There is no time to waste. We do not craft poetry, or a detailed and persuasive treatise based on rich insights and data-driven research into how treacherous the traffic can be at this time of day. We simply yell, "Stop! Get out of the road!"

Fierce love sometimes compels us to issue clear and direct commands. John the Baptist seemed to discern that an urgent moment was at hand that called for terse imperatives. He was all coxswain the whole length of his short, faithful race. If you have ever seen—or been—a coxswain, you know how exhausting and yet how essential the task is.

Crafting a segment of our sermons in the imperative mode can be exhausting for some of us because it lands us in a space we feel ambivalent about, or even downright afraid of. When we think of preachers commanding, recent stories of abusive and bullying pastors spring to mind. We envision pointing fingers and haranguing tirades. Some of us have experienced outright trauma as members of those churches. Leaders to whom we gave credence misused their pulpit or platform. Speakers weaponized imperatives and used them to shame and condemn. The very place we trusted to be a safe space for growth and grace became a setting for authoritarian or manipulative messages. Even if we have not been personally harmed by a toxic leadership culture, we grieve to hear of how it has damaged the body of Christ as a whole.

Some of us experienced stern scolding and harsh commands from parents, spouses, athletic coaches, or employers. These also breed shame and disempowerment. Such tactics never bring about lasting changes since they short-circuit healthy transformation processes. They leave no room for listeners to come to ownership about a course of action. If you received harsh leadership in any of those settings, my prayer is that our gracious God will gently lead you to still waters where you may find healing and restoration for your soul. For some of us, the invitation to embrace the imperative mode in our leadership surfaces a need to explore our histories as recipients of harsh imperatives before we are ready to use them in life-giving ways.

As we learn to use the imperative graciously, it helps to notice *what* the prophets, Jesus, and the apostles commanded. So much of the time, their commands were to do delightful things. It was the spiritual equivalent of being told, "Have some cake!" (After a nourishing meal, of course.) Trust. Delight. Rest. Be of good courage. Be not afraid. Taste and see that the Lord is good. Throughout the biblical narrative, God issued commands from a heart of love. At the outset, God commanded humans to be fruitful, tend well the garden God gave them, and stay away from destructive choices. Commands from the Lord have been an expression of God's kindness since the beginning.

Ideally, they are in our preaching as well. In Eugene Cho's sermon, "Faith and Politics," he reflects insightfully on the challenges of being faithful witnesses in the charged political landscape of the United States today. He peppers his talk with crisp yet kind imperatives. He says, "Be bold and courageous. Yes, we'll find ourselves in tension. Stay Engaged. Remain hopeful. Love anyway. Walk with integrity, and bear witness to Christ."[5] We feel empowered and encouraged as we listen to Cho's words, not harangued.

The second thing we notice is how often a promise undergirded a command, whether it preceded or followed it. In the mindset of the prophets, as they called Israel to return, God was right there on the field, a player-coach wanting Israel to flourish. God in Christ led in the same way with his band of disciples. For example, he paired command with promise as he said, "Do not be afraid, little flock. Your heavenly father has chosen gladly to give you the kingdom" (Luke 12:32).

Andy Crouch pairs assurance and imperative well as he ends a sermon on how our acts of culture-making honor our Creator. He first promises the new creation that God is bringing. Then he says, "Now, go out into this world, to take the good world God has made, that others have already cultivated and made very good, and do your part to shape it, to till it, to keep it, to cultivate, to create in it. Create something that might be called the glory and honor of nations and that will give God glory in his image-bearers."[6]

Some preachers slip too quickly into the imperative before building a foundation of trust from which to do so. Or they use it to ask us to do things that are not in line with the life-giving witness of the gospel. This is impatient and rash leadership. Yet, others of us shy away from it altogether, and that is also a failure of leadership. If we are becoming gentle and yet confident leaders, we will naturally find ourselves entering the imperative mode in nearly every preaching event, if only briefly.

---

5. Cho, "Faith and Politics."
6. Crouch, "Culture Making."

We do so to catalyze life-giving discipleship. The imperative excels at getting people in motion, which can be a tremendous gift when inertia or fear has kept them stuck or spinning in place. Usually, it fits best near the end, as an implication and outgrowth of the truths we described in the indicative mode. We don't bark it as an order but include it as a natural outworking and implication of truths we have proclaimed. On some Sundays, we may command simply to fortify an already existent faithful obedience. We call beloved friends to persist and persevere in the path they are already walking, despite the hardships. We sense a need for more radical changes on other weeks, so we call them to make them with courage and kindness.

Using the Subjunctive Well

The indicative and imperative are at the far ends of the indirect to direct influence spectrum. Might there be a middle ground, stronger than simple description but less forceful than a command? There is. Many languages offer us a fascinating liminal space between the two, called the subjunctive. If you are not familiar with it grammatically, don't worry. It is admittedly a bit nebulous, and we'll unfold its uses as we go.

You've seen it in sentences that begin with these auxiliary verbs: *would, could, should, might, may,* and *shall,* as in, "Shall we dance?" Those words shift the verb that follows them into the subjunctive, though its form often looks the same. Phrases like "I wish," "How about," and "Let's" can signal and trigger that shift into the subjunctive as well. Notice that any sentence beginning with those words or phrases does not describe an existing reality, nor is it commanding. Instead, "Shall we dance?" is *imagining* a future desired reality, one in which you graciously overlook my two left feet and say yes to my daring invitation. And imagining is something we want to do often and well when we preach.

Activating Imagination

The subjunctive at times behaves like the cunning trickster in a play. The trickster or fool subverts and deconstructs our assumptions about what is happening on stage. It enters the game like a wild card, throwing open new possibilities. From years of playing Uno with my sister, I can tell you that things change fast when a wild card comes into play. Sentences using the subjunctive often invite us to travel a different route, as they ask, "What if we *were to* try this instead?" It is the moment my doctor finally finishes scribbling on the examining table paper, looks me in the eye, and asks, "What if you were to get up an hour earlier and exercise every day? Imagine how much more energy you would have all day long and how toned your muscles would be." He invites me to picture a challenging but good new path, to prime my mind and will for action.

This tactic takes one step back from the bold advance of an imperative. Doing so creates what homiletician Sally Brown calls a "rehearsal space"[7] for faithful action in the week ahead. That lets the listener engage with us in a creative and collaborative process. For example, rather than the terse, "I'm warning you!" of chapter 2, it more graciously asks the neighbors, "*Would it be possible* to play your music more quietly after 10 PM?" This question lets the neighbors mentally explore a behavior change and arrive at ownership of it. We can voice the fears and hopes accompanying possible scenarios and actions in the safe rehearsal space of gathered worship.

We often fail to reach for the subjunctive because we lack the patience for the slow process it invites the listener to engage. We can only employ it when we feel we have patience and time. Brown shares this concern. "Too often preachers bypass this crucial step of entertaining possible courses of action." When this happens, she writes, "Listeners have no chance to invest their own imaginative energy in making connections between the biblical text and the realities of their everyday lives."[8]

Speakers who choose it embrace a different kind of leadership, one that is willing to suffer and wait as a process plays out and to risk that their subtler influence gambit may miss altogether.

The subjunctive also highlights what others might miss, as we saw the indicative do above. It does this by asking what we *might* miss or *could* forget or *may* overlook. For example, wise preachers might notice a rush to "get back to normal" and put the pandemic in the rearview mirror. They will ask, "What if gifts might be buried in the rubble of this awful season? What if a moving-on mentality would cause us to miss them?" In Jesus' parable, when the rash servants ask if they should pull up all the weeds in the owner's garden (and move on), the owner says, "No, because while you are pulling up the weeds, you *might* uproot the wheat with them" (Matt 13:29). The owner does not know that this will happen, but it *might*, and he wants to avoid that loss. The subjunctive allows the preacher to ask, "What if in this hard season we have learned new ways to take time for each other, to

---

7. Brown, *Sunday's Sermon*, 96.
8. Brown, *Sunday's Sermon*, 66.

treasure each other even from a distance? What would it look like to carry those lessons with us as we return to greater proximity? Might that make us more willing to go the extra mile to include the elderly and members with special needs? Let's not fail to harvest that lovely wheat in our rush to get back into our buildings."

Playful, prayerful preachers use the subjunctive like a detective dusting for fingerprints. They ask, "What if the Lord's hand were at work *right here*? In the rubble of the pandemic, what if God has been refining, forming, and healing us, and even revealing new facets of God's mercy and compassion?" The prophets did this among the people who had weathered the aching trauma of exile. They had lost so much, from the temple that assured them of God's presence to the land that reminded them of God's favor and gave them the smells and sounds of home. Everything hurt, and the prophets saw how vulnerable they were to idolatry at that moment—just as we all are in times of loss and confusion. Therefore, the prophets spoke words to stir people's imaginations when their mental capacity for imagining had dimmed and atrophied.

They dared to ask, "What if these desiccated bones were to live?" (Ezek 37). "What if gushing streams were to flow in the wasteland?" (Isa 43:19). "What if a joy you cannot fathom in your current pain were to fill your hearts nearly to bursting?" (Isa 54:1). Their prophetic ministry did for the people what Sam Wells hopes a sermon will do: "We come before God naked in our need and limitless in our expectation. That is how the sermon should have left us: completely aware of the reality of our weakness and folly, yet on fire with the wonder of what God can do, even with us."[9]

Leveraging Uncertainty

Commands bring utmost clarity, whereas wild card "what-if" utterances take speaker and listener into uncharted territory. We prefer to lead with bold declarations of what we will most definitely do, but the pandemic has forced us all into a more tentative speech about our plans. We are learning to live in that space, and the subjunctive gives us a tool with which we may still lead from there. For most of us, it is not a mode that comes naturally. With practice, we might just come to enjoy it and conclude that it is how we should have been leading all along.

---

9. Wells, "Teaching Eucharist," 2.

A variation on the subjunctive is a "contrary to fact" statement. It is not a lie or a falsehood. Instead, it is a phrase about a possible future contrary to the facts currently on the ground. These set the stage for warnings or promises about what could happen if a given scenario came to pass. For example, "If it *were* to rain, you *would* be glad to have an umbrella along."

Preacher Hosanna Wong proclaims, "If you were filled with this kind of love—if your foundation of life were based on this kind of love, if everything you were dwelling on were about how loved you are, there just wouldn't be room for your fear."[10] As Wong demonstrates, the subjunctive mode allows us to preach hopeful futures for those we love. We also use it in our narrative work as preachers, for that "contrary to fact" imagining where we invite listeners to enter the life of a biblical character. We ask, "If you were Esther, what would you do if summoned to the banquet?" Of course, you aren't Esther, so the statement is contrary to fact, but the question is well worth asking since all of us have been or one day will be in Esther's shoes, facing a moral dilemma and being called upon to respond with courage and integrity.

Opening phrases such as *I suggest, I wish, I fear, I believe,* and *I hope* also cue a shift into the subjunctive mode. What's striking here is the element of vulnerable testimony these phrases make possible—and require. These phrases insert the speaker's longings and desires into the sentence. If we assert in the indicative, "The weather forecasts a 40 percent chance of rain," and then it rains, we are covered—we can shrug and say, "Well, I guess the forecast was wrong." But if, as friends all clamor to cancel the hike, we venture a subjunctive, "I doubt it will rain," and then it does, our waterlogged friends will rib us for weeks. The stakes are so much higher when we say to a struggling congregation, "I believe God has a bright future for this church." If you have led a small and troubled church, you know that this is not a glib line we throw out without real discernment. I once had to begin to say to a congregation in meetings, "I suggest that we consider closing our doors." Uttering a sentence like this can be brave leadership, though rarely well received.

Breaking Free from Organizational Gridlock

The subjunctive, much like the indicative, participates in reframing. Many congregations are stuck in a present that feels painful. They may be

---

10. Wong, "I Will Not Be Afraid."

understandably fearful that they will cease to exist altogether if their decline continues or clinging to a fantasy about the resurgence that will come after they slap a quick technical fix on the problem. It is nearly impossible to think together fruitfully when these dynamics dominate.

Congregational systems thinker Ed Friedman calls this reality "imaginative gridlock."[11] What do groups need most at that moment? He writes, "For a fundamental reorientation to occur, that spirit of adventure which optimizes serendipity and enables new perceptions . . . must happen first."[12] Have you ever been in a leadership meeting that began in gridlock or bogged down in it midway through, and then something happened to break it loose, allowing everyone present to understand the problem and imagine the future differently? If so, you know how rejuvenating that feels. What you may not have noticed was the way sentences worded in the subjunctive likely helped bring that about.

For example, a subjunctive-form question might break the stalemate in meetings marked by imaginative gridlock. "*Could* we approach this a different way? *Might* we leverage this moment to serve our community? What *would change* if we looked at this from another angle?" As Tod Bolsinger notes, "Reframing allows leaders to see possibilities where others see dead ends; it offers us the tools to break the imaginative gridlock of our situation by considering alternative perspectives."[13] When you need an infusion of a spirit of adventure, the subjunctive is a trustworthy ally.

Preaching from the Middle of the Rubble

It's one thing for a building contractor to tell the laborers to "Get to work!" It's another when Nehemiah, shovel in hand, says, "Let us arise and build!" (Neh 2:18). Nehemiah weeps, prays, learns, and listens, but at the right moment, he stands in the middle of the rubble and exhorts his hearers to action, including himself. Another use of the subjunctive is what is called *hortative* speech. The Latin verb *hortari* means to encourage or urge. The imperative does not include the speaker in the commanded action. However, the hortative subjunctive allows speakers to include themselves as *commanded* even as they command. They are not above being led even as they lead. So, when pastors say, "Let's work hard together this year to make

---

11. Friedman, *Failure of Nerve*, 29.
12. Friedman, *Failure of Nerve*, 33.
13. Bolsinger, *Canoeing the Mountains*, 208.

this vision a reality," and then share what they are risking or trying differently to do that, we want to sign up.

Praying and Blessing

Finally, the subjunctive often gives us language for our public prayers, where we express audacious hopes for others or ourselves, hopes we could never bring to pass on our own. The subjunctive allows us to dream big dreams and then entrust them to a God powerful enough to receive those requests and bring them to pass. When Paul prays for the Ephesians in the first round (Eph 1:17–18), he asks that God *give them the Spirit to know* him and that the eyes of their hearts *may be* enlightened. When he takes up prayer again, he asks that God *may strengthen* them so that Christ *may dwell* in them, so that they *may have power* and *may be filled* to the measure of all the fullness of God (Eph 3:14–19). He ends by asking them to pray for him. His request is the cry of a preacher, also worded in the subjunctive. He asks for their prayers that words *may be given* to him (Eph 6:19).

The subjunctive also lends us language with which to bless. When Paul closes his first letter to the Thessalonians, an appeal to holy living, he runs through a terse list of roughly seventeen imperatives (Encourage! Help! Be kind!), culminating in the stark command to "Stay away from every evil." Surely, they would be all set if they obeyed all seventeen of these commands. But Paul goes on, shifting into the subjunctive: "Now *may* the God of peace himself make you completely holy and may your spirit and soul and body be kept entirely blameless at the coming of our Lord Jesus Christ." They need imperatives catalyzing them to pursue practices that will keep them from harm, strengthen their community, and give them life. But their deeds are not enough, so Paul blesses them with the presence of Christ. He commits his flock to the care of God and implores God to act powerfully on their behalf.

I find that subjunctive speech does not come naturally for many of us. Few of us have seen it modeled well. So, when we want to influence, we reach for the imperative, thinking it is the most direct way of exerting influence. It takes patience and practice to expand our repertoire to include questions and "what if we . . ." statements that invite imagination, insert ourselves into the appeal, and bring our prayers into the conversation.

Learning to use all three verbal modes deftly is not just a matter of speaking well but of doing the inner work needed so that your speech resonates with who you are becoming as a leader and flows from a wise and loving heart. May the Lord bless you as you do that good work.

Ask This:

- Pull up a recent sermon and look at the modes of the verbs. What are you best at doing? Describing to highlight, honor, and reframe? Commanding to catalyze change? Exhorting and imagining?
- Which mode is the hardest for you to use effectively? What might that reflect about where you are in your journey as a leader?
- What could you try in your upcoming sermon to strengthen your weak hand?

Try This:

- Twice this month, find something your congregation or a member of it does well and honor that publicly.
- Practice inserting imagining moments into a few sermons soon. For example, how would you finish these sentences in a sermon:
    1. "What if for the next six months we were to try doing _____?"
    2. "What if we were to see this setback as an opportunity, a chance to _____?"
    3. "What if God is using this time to shape us as people who could _____?"

9

Preacher as Catalyst

Sparking Transformation in the Active and Passive Voice

"You are being sent forth to be the church in the world. What we do here in adoring God is connected to the action you will engage in as worship of God in all you do. You are not alone in this. As God is present in our gathering, so God will be with us in our homes, neighborhoods, schools, and workplaces. God go with you and empower you for the mission that lies before you. God keep you safe and strong, committed, and focused, filled with faith and love. Go in peace. Serve the Lord."

—CLAYTON SCHMIT

HUMAN CHANGE IS MYSTERIOUS. Sometimes a friend's capacity for quick and durable transformation takes our breath away. On rare but glorious days, even our capacity to walk a new path can startle and delight us. I have heard converts testify that a desperate craving for harmful substances simply fell away when they converted—and it never returned. I believe them, and I rejoice. But I also know people, myself included, who have wrestled for decades with lesser demons that cling to our spirits like ticks to skin. The Scriptures are replete with the stories of people making radical changes and subtle, incremental ones. Sometimes those happen instantaneously, and sometimes they unfold "with wandering steps and slow,"[1] as the poet John Milton poignantly described it.

The Bible depicts a God who takes great interest in the process of human change. God often initiates changes through visions, angelic announcements, or human messengers. God doggedly stays with his people as they struggle to live out the implications of his truths and ways. Throughout the Scriptures, we see God lamenting the losses and celebrating the gains alongside the humans God created. While God is highly involved from the start to the finish of human transformation, God also leaves open a wide sphere of human agency and freedom. God makes space for us to participate in (or thwart) change processes at significant levels. The choices and efforts we make matter. The struggles and barriers are real. Leaders who attend well to the complexities of human hearts, beginning with their own, will be more able to speak into those deep places within us of resistance to change. That insight and empathy will equip them to teach us how Christ's grace forms us. They will be able to promise us God's presence with us, as pastor and theologian Clayton Schmit's powerful words of sending above do. Our final chapter will explore how our preached words enter the confluence of God's renewing work and humanity's effortful engagement in response to God's activity.

From the outset, I invite you to lead others toward transformation as one who unashamedly admits your own deep need and actively pursues and gratefully receives transformation. Young adulthood experts Kara Powell and Steven Argue begin their winsome and wise parenting book, *Growing With*, on a striking note. They urge parents to view their vocation of parenting as "a mutual journey of intentional growth for both parent and child that trusts God to transform us all."[2] I love that. It articulates what I hope for in the relationship between congregations and their preachers—not that we view congregations as children and pastors as parents—but that we view ministry as a shared and intentional developmental journey. We can better live and lead amidst our congregations when we are confident God has placed us with these specific people to bring about needed change within us.

---

1. Milton, in the closing lines of *Paradise Lost*, depicts Adam and Eve's faltering journey out of Eden, writing, "They hand in hand with wandering steps and slow, Through Eden took their solitary way." Milton, *Paradise Lost*, Book 12.

2. Powell and Argue, *Growing With*, 12.

Preacher as Catalyst

When we look at the language biblical leaders used to stir change, it shows a potent blend of human and divine initiative. Sadly, some of our preaching efforts do not. They either depict humans as nearly inert recipients of God's work or as the only actors on the stage, with God having exited stage left after handing us the script. This chapter asks you to take an unflinching look at the implicit theology of transformation that your sermons reveal. That look under the hood may unearth more than faulty theology; it may point us to needed healing and renewal within us. Frustrating seasons of stymied change in ourselves or others may have left us deeply discouraged. That is understandable, but if you let it go unexamined and untended, it will morph into a cynical apathy that will render you ineffective and unhappy in ministry. Wise leaders will regularly seek the help of spiritual directors, therapists, and trusted friends. One of the most important things those partners do for pastors is validate their pain, allowing them to grieve their losses and disappointments. As we walk this shared journey toward healing and transformation with our congregations, one last bit of grammar will frame our discussion. Let's look at the voice of the verb.

Pity the passive voice. It gets a bad rap in every blog about writing well. In addition, since we contrast it with the active voice, we can think that not much is *happening* in a passive-voice sentence. Far from it. The passive voice gives us a language to express gifts and actions that we receive. Here, we will use the shorthand of the active voice to represent human initiative in change and the passive voice to express God's work. *We act as we are acted upon.* These are always intertwined in the life of faithful discipleship. Of course, we often construct sentences depicting and proclaiming God's work in the active voice, with God as the subject. However, my goal is to give you a memorable paradigm you can use to strength-test your sermon. To help you remember that the passive voice is where you check for your depiction of the work of God, I encourage you to memorize that simple sentence: "We act as we are acted upon." Notice how these biblical authors depict the work of God towards people in the passive voice.

- My frame was not hidden from you when I *was being made* in secret, intricately woven in the depths of the earth. (Ps 139:15)
- Your guilt *is blotted out*. (Isa 6:7)
- Much more surely then, now that *we have been justified* by his blood, *will we be saved* through him from the wrath of God. (Rom 5:9)

- But *you were washed, you were sanctified, you were justified* in the name of the Lord Jesus Christ and in the Spirit of our God. (1 Cor 6:11)
- All of them *were filled* with the Holy Spirit and began to speak in other languages, as the Spirit gave them ability. (Acts 2:4)
- When Jesus saw their faith, he said to the paralytic, "Son, your sins *are forgiven*." (Mark 2:5)
- For by grace, *you have been saved* through faith, and this is not your own doing; it is the gift of God. (Eph 2:8)

When we ask of our sermons, "Do they preach enough passive voice?" we are drilling into our proclamation of God as the author and agent of transformation. We check their clarity about the reality that we humans are finite creatures who look to God in prayerful dependence for every change we seek. Some of us swim in theological streams that place almost all the emphasis on God's work. In these traditions, transformation happens to us entirely at God's hand; our role is simply to welcome it, receive it, and give God grateful praise for it. As British pastor Alan Redpath put it, "Give up the struggle and the fight; relax in the omnipotence of the Lord Jesus; look up into his lovely face, and as you behold him, he will transform you into his likeness. You do the beholding—he does the transforming."[3] Redpath was essentially correct, but many of us have experienced that the line from beholding to transformed practices is not a straight or a short one. Even as we behold the loveliness of Christ, we find ourselves hungry for concrete help in our struggles to live faithfully.

Therefore, we must also ask, "Did my sermon preach change in the active voice? Did it make space for human agency and practical next steps? Did it speak with insight into how we begin a change of habit or heart and why we so often fail to persist in it?" Some of us live out our faith in more activist traditions that focus on our repentant and energetic obedience, whether that leads to ever greater personal holiness or engagement serving our communities and confronting injustices. This emphasis will lead to more active-voice preaching—go, do, strive, serve. Sermons that constantly skew toward one focus or the other are problematic for listeners and preachers alike. Rather than preaching one at the complete neglect of the other, how can we hold these truths in creative tension?

3. Redpath, "Thinking Upon Jesus," https://deeperchristian.com/thinking-upon-jesus-alan-redpath/.

Preacher as Catalyst

Church historian Mark Granquist rightly notes that part of the issue is clarity about where we start. He writes,

> We need to improve ourselves, and we need to improve our world. But if we start with these elements, they are hopelessly doomed to failure, as our old sinful selves cannot do the tasks that we set out for ourselves. Holiness is not ours; it is God's. The only hope we have for holiness is if it comes to us as a gift through the Spirit of God. It is amazing the energy and commitment that such a realization invariably unleashes, as Christians throw off the shackles of self-justification or despair and simply work for the renewal of their lives and God's world.[4]

Granquist roots transformation in the work and character of God, but from there, he makes space for human endeavors we undertake with focused energy and joy. When preaching emphasizes divine agency without ever addressing the dynamics that foster change on the ground or the destructive dynamics that keep humans from changing, we miss an opportunity to equip our listeners to flourish. In a season where choices have been so curtailed and so much feels out of our control, it is good news that we still have the agency to take up habits that bear beautiful fruit. We can choose contentment, generosity, and integrity. If we have cultivated practices that lead to death, we can turn toward life-giving ones. Some of us need to strengthen our active-voice preaching, urging listeners to pursue new pathways, forgive, and extend themselves to care for each other. We need generous helpings of both voices today.

When we preach change, our linguistic choices inevitably flow from our understanding of how fundamentally *possible* meaningful change is—for the hardened criminal or the deeply depressed, the complacent, and the complicit. The gospel invites us to be both clear-eyed and childlike in our hope for others. Moreover, the language we use surfaces other crucial questions about *how* change occurs. What external environmental conditions and internal capacities make change more likely to begin and last? What roles do desire for the good and disgust at the damage, and confession and lament regarding our sinful tendencies, play in propelling us forward? Does identity reformation precede or follow behavioral change? How significant a role does the simple presence of a friend or a caring community play in an individual's capacity to turn from a death-dealing habit? We will explore five aspects of human change—desire, damage, loss, identity, and

---

4. Granquist, "Sanctification and All That," 342.

solidarity—with an eye to how preaching in the active and the passive voice can catalyze transformation.

Human Change

Our tour of human change dynamics will build upon an extended analogy.[5] Imagine that you have lived for years in a gloomy shack in a jungle. Life consists of a daily trip to a stinking, putrid garbage dump. The destination is always dismal, but the path is comfortingly familiar. A trusted old friend shows up one morning as you are setting out on your regular trek to misery and tells you that if you were to hack a new path in a different direction, you would arrive at a stunningly beautiful beach. (Let's assume you're a beach person.) Your friend describes gorgeous sunsets, dolphins eager to frolic with you in warm, clear water, and a scrumptious buffet spread out daily on tables on the sand. This friend hands you a machete and invites you to begin forging that new path.

Close your eyes and imagine yourself at that moment. What do you do? And why? Why might you hesitate or resist? What questions will you want to be answered before you begin? I believe that your choice to forge a new path and to persist at it when your arms are scratched and weary will depend on whether, as you hear your friend's words, something clicks for you around each of these five aspects of change dynamics.

Desire

Here is the crucial question: Did their words spark a longing or hunger within you as you listened to your friend? The desire for something better lies at the heart of every change process. Desire is the forward-propelling, catalytic energy that overcomes initial fears and hesitance. As J. K. A. Smith puts it, "Our wants and longings and desires are at the core of our identity, the wellspring from which our actions and behavior flow."[6] Attraction compels us. Perhaps the friend in the jungle knows that you used to love going to the beach, so he or she can appeal to *memory* as a source of desire. Maybe your friend knows that you have tried before but never made it to the coast, so they must use evocative descriptions to help you imagine what you have never seen and encouragement to overcome your fears of failure.

---

5. Dr. Suzanne Shaw, email with author, June 8, 2021.
6. Smith, *You Are What You Love*, 2.

We see Martin Luther King Jr. drawing upon desire and imagination with his vivid description of an America that has not yet existed. "With this faith, we will be able to hew out of the mountain of despair a stone of hope. With this faith, we will be able to transform the jangling discords of our nation into a beautiful symphony of brotherhood. With this faith, we will be able to work together, to pray together, to struggle together, to go to jail together, to stand up for freedom together, knowing that we will be free one day."[7] He kindles desire with rich metaphor and bold promise, using them to motivate his listeners to forge a new pathway for their nation. He majors in the active voice, describing the work we humans must do to bring about change, but the note of promise of God's work comes in as he says, "we *will* be free one day." This liberation will be the work of God Almighty, whom he thanks as his sonorous speech ends. King was soberly aware that ultimately only God would bring that freedom.

As preachers to listeners who sometimes get stuck on destructive pathways, we will do better at kindling desire if we have spent quality time at the beach ourselves, basking in its beauty. King was embedded in a beloved community that gave him glimpses of the just and reconciling society he imagined for his nation, so that he could describe it with integrity. As we engage in the work of kindling desire, we do so in the glad knowledge that the Holy Spirit is hovering over that work from start to finish, gently whispering the right words in our ears and warmly beckoning listeners through those words.

King's words are a stellar example of active-voice preaching that kindles desire. How might passive-voice preaching do the same? It would likely be worded in the future tense, awakening longing for the work God promises to do in us that we have not yet seen realized. We need to hear God's past work declared over us, but desires are for what we don't yet possess. As we consider our puny strength for hacking new paths to beaches, we need to hear, "You will be made strong by the Holy Spirit for the tasks ahead of you. You will be provided for as you set out on this journey. You will be given what you need to endure it and complete it."

Damage

Imagine that as you stand there contemplating whether the hacking project will be worth the effort, your friend adds, "Listen! There has been a

---

7. King, "I Have a Dream."

massive cholera outbreak at the garbage dump! You simply cannot go there any longer. The disease is heading here, so you must forge a way out of the jungle." You would be much likelier to pick up the machete and get to work, as challenging as it is to do so. Compelling leaders overcome inertia in their hearers by clearly demonstrating that the status quo is no longer a viable option. As Shaw writes, "We name the distress people are in, the desperation they feel, the sorrow under the surface, the frustration with life as it currently is. We lay bare the damage, the costs of behavior or inaction. This is not working. This is not a thriving life."[8]

The formula for effectiveness here is urgency plus empathy. For example, in a funeral sermon to a congregation devastated by the loss of a baby in their midst, preacher Craig Barnes sees potential harm ahead for listeners. He names their pain with compassion as he writes, "Today we are mourning the loss of this precious baby who was taken from us before we were ready to let him go." But then he issues a striking warning, something we don't expect in a funeral sermon. He senses an urgent danger in this painful moment. "Don't dare try to grieve without believing the heavenly Father has received Casey into his eternal arms, or you will never survive the loss. If you choose to resent the loss, your heart will eventually turn dark, and you will be unable to love anything in life. But if in time, you choose to give thanks for the gifts Casey brought into our lives, you will discover that some of his childlike tenderness has been left behind in your own heart."[9] He clarifies the damage that could come to his grieving listeners while expressing his care and hopes for them.

Barnes models active-voice preaching about potential damage or harm to our hearts to catalyze a change in outlook. Passive-voice preaching here might speak of God's work in the past and the ongoing implications that it holds for us. "Disease is rampant at the garbage dump. But you have been rescued from that. You have been liberated and rescued from it, so no longer return there. As Paul exhorted the Galatians, 'Do not let yourselves be burdened again by a yoke of slavery' (Gal 5:1)."

Integration of Loss

Whenever we take a step towards a desired change, we set in motion the formation of new neural pathways. Thankfully, our brains have a tremendous

---

8. Shaw, email with author, June 8, 2021.
9. Barnes, "Casey William Alley," 7.

capacity to do this over time, if not easily or quickly. Those pathways need to be integrated into our current working mental map. Part of how that happens is an acknowledgment of the losses involved in any change. Let's imagine that the cholera outbreak is not so imminent, so you have a bit of time to sit on a log and share with your friend about what it is that draws you to the garbage dump.

It has its charms, after all. You reveal that you were recently elected chief sorter of bottles. It is a coveted title, and it came with no small amount of praise for your excellent sorting skills. "But at the beach," you fret aloud. "I'll have no status or title at all." And besides, you add wistfully, "I worked so hard to clear that path." As we walk with our people through change processes, we must help them acknowledge how they benefit even from destructive patterns and practices. In preaching, this often comes as we preach the narratives of characters like Naaman the leper fulminating about the superiority of his country's rivers, Jonah fleeing God's command, and Simon Peter resisting getting his feet washed. We trace their faltering steps and let them hold up mirrors to our resistances. We all struggle to let go of the small rewards our distorted narratives and practices afford us.

When we encourage people to let go of familiar paths that perhaps once worked but no longer do, we should expect resistance. Often the change seems so obviously better from our vantage point that we are genuinely surprised by the opposition that we meet. I once pastored a church that needed to die. Sunday services were no longer life-giving to anyone involved. Nearly everyone agreed that the best option would be to go as a group to join a nearby, vibrant church that had enthusiastically invited them to do just that. But one woman vehemently resisted. Betty stood at the center of every activity this little church still mustered, even well into her eighties. In a conversation on the church patio, she agreed with all my persuasive logic but, in the end, ruefully murmured, "But I'd be nobody there." How had I missed it? Betty was not being stubborn. Instead, she was terrified. I had failed to name the losses and come alongside her as she faced and integrated them. As the poet Anatole France reminds us, "All changes, even the most longed for, have their melancholy; for what we leave behind us is a part of ourselves; we must die to one life before we can enter another."[10]

It takes enormous courage to let go of what comforts us and fortifies our identity, even if that source of comfort is ultimately destructive. After

10. France, cited in https://thepastorsworkshop.com/sermon-quotes-list-of-topics/.

all, the proposed benefit of the new path is only hypothetical; we cannot yet see it. But the loss is smack dab in front of us—it was all Betty could see. Change involves not only the risk of loss but the certainty of it. It is highly vulnerable to lay down what has yielded safe and predictable outcomes, hoping that a new course of action could make space for a different reality to emerge. If we don't acknowledge this in our preaching, we will lose credibility. As a pastor and preacher, if you understand that every change process is messy and challenging, you'll help us lament the losses and do the integration work that makes change possible. You'll urge us to extend grace and patience to ourselves and each other even as you strongly encourage us to turn from what is harming us.

Active-voice preaching that lets us integrate losses will include the compassionate naming of the challenges and the firm promise of God's presence with us as we endure them. Pastor and writer Noel Snyder does this well in a sermon for Palm Sunday. "As followers of Jesus, we learn to become living sacrifices. We learn that our entire lives are subject to redefinition, to revision, to crucifixion even, so that God may bring about something much bigger than we could ever imagine."[11]

Passive-voice preaching that has named losses well often ends in promise. "As you let go of what comforted you in the past, know that you are held, cherished, and sustained by the God of peace."

Identity and Purpose

Let's imagine that those dolphins at the beach are suffering from an odd flipper affliction, and your friend knows that before you fell into your garbage fixation, you were an accomplished aquatic veterinarian. (Who knew?) Your friend appeals to you to enter that identity and vocation anew. A potent call to change nearly always appeals to identity. In some cultures, identity is found primarily in one's work; in others, it puts down its roots in the family and groups to which one belongs. A strong indicator of our identity is where and with whom we spend our disposable time and energy. These choices not only reveal what we love and who we hope to become, but they shape our loves and hopes as well. Our practices form us even as our desired identity informs our actions in an iterative process. Sometimes our sense of identity is distorted by lies from our culture and by shaming messages from our families of origin. Sometimes a significant failure in life

---

11. Snyder, *Sermons that Sing*, 168.

crushes a positive conception of ourselves. One of our greatest privileges as preachers is reminding people of who they are in Christ, how God sees and treasures them, and how that restored identity can free them to walk more life-giving paths.

Effective preachers motivate change by describing who people will become as they embrace new habits and attitudes. Sometimes we do that by highlighting the beauty in the lives of ordinary saints from Scripture or the global history of the church. We invite our listeners to identify as a member of that strange company. Jesus often sealed a change process such as healing with a statement about identity, which for him was bound up with belonging to the family of God. After Zacchaeus announced his intention to give away his money, Jesus publicly named him a son of Abraham (Luke 19:9). After Jesus sets a woman free of an ailment that had oppressed her for years, he publicly calls her a daughter of Abraham (Luke 13:16). Their identity would come from finding their names within a sacred family tree. Jesus transformed identities marked by shame to ones permeated with honor and value and marked by membership in a big family. These words of blessing and belonging rang in their ears as they lived into their new identities. A solid identity and sense of belonging give us courage and grit to persist and press through the setbacks. We can get up after we have stumbled when we know who and whose we are.

Active-voice preaching around identity may paint a stark contrast between two paths through life. For example, in a sermon on Mark 10:46–52, the story of Bartimaeus, Barnes says,

> The text today offers us two options. Either you can ask Jesus for help with your crusade to achieve more, a crusade that will inevitably leave your life filled with disappointment and complaint because once you make achieving the goal, you will never have enough. Or you can ask for the mercy that comes when one prays to receive their life. Not to achieve it, but to receive it. If you make that your mission, to receive your life from the merciful savior, then your constant companion is gratitude because you are now paying attention to the blessings only a savior can give you.[12]

How might passive-voice preaching form and reinforce the new identity given to us by Jesus Christ? To paraphrase Schmit's words of sending for concluding a worship service, we might say as we end, "You are being sent forth to be faithful disciples in the world. God will be with you in your

---

12. Barnes, sermon preached at the Washington National Cathedral, October 25, 2015, https://www.youtube.com/watch?v=4a_UFhT3aCY.

homes, neighborhoods, schools, and workplaces. You will be led and empowered by God for the mission that lies before you. You will be kept safe and strong, committed, and focused, filled with courage and love."

Solidarity

What your old friend in the jungle has asked you to do is hard. But how different would it feel if they pulled out another machete (in a friendly way, of course) and said, "Did you think I was going to leave you to do this alone? No! I will work alongside you. Let's forge this path together." That would certainly help me to begin. It would help me persist, too. Jesus lived out radical solidarity with his disciples and suffering people in his life on earth. He promises it to us today in the form of the Holy Spirit, the Paraclete who comes alongside to guide, sustain, and encourage. More tangibly, God has made solidarity one of the core vocations of the body of Christ. God calls us to cheer on every member's effort to embrace a new way of relating to others or forego a harmful one. Preachers are the enthusiastic mascots on the floor leading the cheering. We unabashedly celebrate the work God is doing. As we do so, we build and sustain the forward momentum of our faith communities. And we are changed in the process.

When we enter radical partnerships with others in need of change, our own needs bubble up to the surface. In my work with adults with disabilities, I repeatedly saw that their fears—and the frustrating behaviors they engaged in as a result—were usually just more honest expressions of the same fears lurking within me. Caring for them was crucial to my transformation journey. I may not have squirreled away food in odd corners of my bedroom out of fear of going hungry in the night, but I was stingy with my time when a friend needed help, out of a silly fear of not finishing my day's to-do list. We are all drawn to the garbage dump on some days. Honesty about the muck inside us lets us enter into empathetic solidarity with others.

We see this process of mutual transformation strikingly in the book of Acts. The apostles are being changed as they proclaim and lead. The Holy Spirit is at work *in* the apostles in nearly as many scenes as the Spirit works through them. The Spirit sends them down unfamiliar roads and into uncomfortable places to transform their perceptions of insiders and outsiders, sharpen their capacity to listen to the voice of the risen Christ, and deepen their dependence on God. As Peter processed and eventually acted on the vision of God's gifts poured out on Gentiles, his heart expanded. Peter needed Cornelius, the Roman centurion to whom God sent him to preach, as much as Cornelius needed Peter (Acts 10).

What active-voice preaching looks like here is proclaiming vision and hope that our communities can become centers of radical solidarity with each other. "What we are up to is hard. We seek to live against the grain of the culture around us, and we will need each other to do that. If we choose to know and be known, rejoice with each other's victories and mourn each other's defeats, we will go further. Let's commit to that."

What passive-voice preaching looks like here would be emphasizing the generosity of God in giving us the Holy Spirit and the body of Christ. "You have not been asked to walk this road alone. The risen Christ walks it with you, and in the church, you have been given a rich company of fellow travelers."

Conclusion

We have looked at five factors that help individuals or groups successfully pivot away from harm and towards life. We who lead others endeavor to spark desire, heighten awareness of damage, help people integrate losses, cultivate new identity and purpose, and shape communities where we come alongside each other. This consideration of how humans change has sought to name the work of God in each of these areas. The Holy Spirit is ultimately the one who awakens and purifies desire within us and convicts us of the harm our sin does to our loved ones and our souls. Jesus is our Emmanuel, God with us as we integrate the losses involved in change and receive a new identity. The Father "from whom every family derives its name" (Eph 3:15) is the creator of the families and communities that give us the sense of belonging we need to change. While it is good news that we humans have agency, it is far better news that God does. As the seventh-century theologian and abbot Paschasius Radbertus proclaimed, "Christ is held by the hand of hope. We hold him and are held. But it is a greater good that we are held by Christ than that we hold him. For we can hold him only so long as we are held by him."[13]

A close look at our language may reveal an underlying belief that we will prevail if we simply try harder and do more. By contrast, Pasquarello notes how robust confidence in God's work will enliven our preaching. He

13. Radbertus, *De Fe, Spe, et Charite*, Liber II, Caput I.

writes, "Preaching will be an act of praise that summons listeners to become glad recipients of the generous outpouring of self-giving love by the crucified and risen Lord, the one who speaks and acts in the fullness of the Spirit's power."[14] Ultimately, Pasquarello is right; this is where the emphasis should land. When it does, our sermons become doxological; they catalyze worship. We are creatures called to live in glad response to our creator.

Disconcertingly, a close look at the change narratives running through our preaching may also lay bare our discouragement. It has been a tough season all around, and it would be surprising if we were not somewhat discouraged as we emerge from it. This chapter extends an invitation to acknowledge and confess your frustration and disappointment as you look at wished-for changes in yourself, your siblings, your children, and your congregants. Honest lament can prevent us from sliding into cynicism or despair. You inevitably bring the sorrows you have lived through into your preaching, so it is worth taking a hard look at what they have cost you and what you are carrying. Lament that in the presence of God and get all the help you need to heal. Do that because it is intrinsically worth doing, but also so you can preach for change with integrity.

Ask This:

Survey your last four or so sermons, ferreting out the meta-narrative of change found within them.

- Does your preaching express subtle, underlying pessimism about your listener's capacity to change or that of the congregation as a whole? Or do you proclaim a robust faith in God's power to transform us?
- Do you overpromise us that change will happen instantaneously, without costs or setbacks?
- Is your preaching skewed heavily toward active-voice preaching that emphasizes human effort to try harder and do more or toward passive-voice sermons that leave little space for human agency?
- Do you show insight into the dynamics of human change processes, such as the need to cultivate desire, highlight damage, integrate losses, sharpen identity in Christ, and call us to come alongside each other?

---

14. Pasquarello, *We Speak*, 48.

Try This:

If you notice an overemphasis in one direction or the other, try reading Christian authors and listening to preachers whose emphasis is firmly in the other direction. Notice what they do well and what makes their preaching effective. Then, let that season and strengthen your preaching.

Conclusion

THIS BOOK DOES NOT come with a guarantee, much as in some ways I wish it could. It is a paradigm that you may use similarly to how those in various professions use a checklist. While checklists improve outcomes, they can never account for every factor. A surgical team could tick off every item on the pre-operating checklist without attaining a successful outcome, since a slight wavering of the knife could prove to be a fatal error. Or a patient may be in such poor overall health that she does not survive the surgery, despite the team's flawless execution of every detail. The same is true of our preaching. I wish I could promise you that if you look closely at the verbs in your sermon and find the perfect balance of your use of person, tense, mode, and voice, your sermon would succeed in the best sense of that word.

The truth is, we never fully know how or why a sermon finds good soil in which to land. For example, God worked a miraculous and large-scale turning of human hearts from the four-word sermon of a recalcitrant preacher (Jonah). In contrast, Jeremiah's faithful, eloquent words seemed to yield little results over decades. But at least one person was transformed by Jeremiah's words. That person was Jeremiah. We see him grow in tenacity, gritty trust in the Lord, and even love for his people as he preaches to them.

I encourage you to view the faithful voicing of each of these verb forms as a way of living out the journey of discipleship with the people you love and lead. Let each one form an invitation to grow and receive from God and preach more effectively. As we come to the end of our exploration of how the intentional and effective use of verbs can foster a deep connection with those who hear and respond to our sermons, let me close with an extended blessing to you as you lean into new ways of speaking truth.

As you *testify*, bringing yourself fully to every sermon, may that grow trust in God to protect you when you expose your weaknesses. As you take brave risks in this area, you will grow in humility and freedom. You will come to depend on God alone for your reputation. Your ability to share your struggles will nurture a culture of grace and a community of people who are glad to be creatures—finite, in process, and turned in grateful hope toward their Creator. Finally, your willingness to be a fellow traveler who is still learning what Scripture means and how God works will model freedom, curiosity, and humility for your listeners.

May God bless your efforts to *host* your listeners, inviting them to feast upon God's word with joyful reverence. May that practice shape you into a more generous and gracious person, one whose table is wide, and whose heart is open.

May the bold speech where you *directly address us* grow strong leadership muscles in you. Proclamation is exciting. It brings us into intimate partnership with the promise-making God. May your faith and delight in God grow as you dare to speak beautiful truth straight to us.

May your fresh and resonant proclamation of our good God inspire you to worship, both as you prepare and as you preach. Don't be afraid to be visibly moved as you declare the word. Let us see your love for God. As you publicly live out your worship before your church, may that practice deepen wonder, trust, and delight within you.

May the pursuit of *wisdom* for yourself and your faith community be a gift to them.

Pursuing virtues and turning from vices has led many Christians down paths of self-righteousness, anxiety, and the relentless pursuit of merit. May this not be so for you and the people you love and lead. Instead, may the search be marked at every turn by Christ's grace, so that it makes you humbler and more enjoyable to be around.

May you find immense joy as a *storyteller* of Scripture's narratives. May that practice foster a lively shared memory of God's past deeds. May those retold tales shape your listeners into fearless, generous, and wholehearted disciples.

May the work you do to grow a community of *discernment* form you as a patient listener. May asking the questions of what God is up to now become a life-giving spiritual discipline, one where you sense the lively and kind work of the Holy Spirit even in the hardest of circumstances.

May your preaching of *hope* deepen your hope. May you find the strength to carry hope when it feels heavy and, paradoxically, may hope lift and sustain you. Never give in to the temptation to preach false and

Conclusion

hyped-up hope to your people. But never fail to risk proclaiming the foolishness and childlikeness of gospel hope.

May your growth in savvy use of modes of *influence*, from commanding to inviting and describing, give you boldness where you need to risk and restraint where you need gentleness.

May your invitations to *transformation* be rooted in the initiative of God and yet rooted as well in awareness of the dynamics that make human change hard yet possible. May God give you patience when the rate of change in the people you lead is ever so much slower than you desire. So much may be transpiring beneath the surface, just about to break through the soil. As you stay with them in those messy processes, much growth may be happening within you as well.

May the preaching you do, in whatever context you find yourself, find resonance with your listeners as you sound notes that resonate faithfully with Scripture and the character of our good and beautiful God.

Bibliography

Alston, Wallace M., Jr. "The Recovery of Theological Preaching." In *The Power to Comprehend with All the Saints: The Formation and Practice of a Pastor-Theologian*, edited by Wallace Alston and Cynthia Jarvis, 221–36. Grand Rapids: Eerdmans, 2009.

Alston, Wallace M., Jr., and Cynthia Jarvis, eds. *The Power to Comprehend with All the Saints: The Formation and Practice of a Pastor-Theologian*. Grand Rapids: Eerdmans, 2009.

Anderson, Ray. *The Shape of Practical Theology: Empowering Ministry with Theological Praxis*. Downers Grove, IL: InterVarsity, 2001.

Augustine of Hippo. *Expositions of the Psalms*, vol. 6. Oxford: J. H. Parker, 1847–1857.

Barnes, Craig. "Casey William Alley." In *This Incomplete One: Words Occasioned by the Death of a Young Person*, edited by Michael D. Bush, 3–8. Grand Rapids: Eerdmans, 2006.

Bolsinger, Tod. *Canoeing the Mountains: Christian Leadership in Uncharted Territory*. Downers Grove, IL: InterVarsity, 2018.

Bridges, William, and Susan Bridges. *Managing Transitions: Making the Most of Change*. Boston: Da Capo, 2016.

Brown, Peter. *Augustine of Hippo: A Biography*. Berkeley: University of California Press, 2000.

Brown, Sally. *Sunday's Sermon for Monday's World: Preaching to Shape Daring Witness*. Grand Rapids: Eerdmans, 2020.

Buechner, Frederick. *Beyond Words: Daily Readings in the ABCs of Faith*. New York: Harper Collins, 2009.

———. *Telling the Truth: The Gospel as Tragedy, Comedy, and Fairy Tale*. San Francisco: Harper & Row, 1977.

Burns, James MacGregor. *Leadership*. New York: Open Road Media, 2012.

Cho, Eugene. "Faith and Politics." Sermon preached at Sanctuary Church, July 26, 2020. https://www.youtube.com/watch?v=4PnxqTt4ekk.

Crouch, Andy. "Culture Making: The Good News in a Changing World." Sermon preached at Biola University, June 18, 2013. https://www.youtube.com/watch?v=JTT6Wshs7NQ.

Davis, Ellen F. *Wondrous Depth: Preaching the Old Testament*. Louisville: Westminster John Knox, 2005.

Dickinson, Emily. *Complete Poems of Emily Dickinson*. Boston: Little, Brown, 1960.

Dronke, Peter, ed. *Nine Medieval Latin Plays*. Cambridge Medieval Classics 1. Cambridge: Cambridge University Press, 1995.

Edwards, O. C., Jr. *A History of Preaching*. Nashville: Abingdon, 2004.

Bibliography

Florence, Anna Carter. *Preaching as Testimony.* Louisville: Westminster John Knox, 2007.

Forsyth, P. T. "The One Great Preacher." In *The Company of Preachers: Wisdom on Preaching from Augustine to the Present,* edited by Richard Lischer, 411–16. Grand Rapids: Eerdmans, 2002.

Friedman, Edwin H. *A Failure of Nerve: Leadership in the Age of the Quick Fix.* New York: Church Publishing, 1999.

Gonzalez, Justo. *Essential Theological Terms.* Louisville: Westminster John Knox, 2005.

Gordon, Carolyn. "Fighting the Good Fight." Sermon preached for Calvin Symposium on Christian Worship, 2013. https://worship.calvin.edu/resources/resource-library/symposium-2013-forgiveness/.

Granquist, Mark. "Sanctification and All That." *Word and World* 40.4 (Fall 2020) 341–42.

Greco, Dorothy Littell. "Reflections on COVID-19, Week Two: Idolatry." *Words and Images* (blog). https://www.dorothygreco.com/reflections-on-covid-19-week-two-idolatry.

Hauerwas, Stanley. "Why Time Cannot and Should not Heal the Wounds of History but Time has Been and can be Redeemed." *Scottish Journal of Theology* 53.1 (2000) 33–49.

Heath, Chip, and Dan Heath. *Switch: How to Change Things When Change Is Hard.* New York: Penguin Random House, 2010.

Hendrix, John. "Making the Trip in Imagination and Memory." *Review and Expositor* 86 (1989) 417–29.

Jensen, Richard. *Telling the Story: Variety and Imagination in Preaching.* Minneapolis: Augsburg Fortress, 1980.

Katangole, Emmanuel. *Born from Lament: The Theology and Politics of Hope in Africa.* Grand Rapids: Eerdmans, 2017.

King, Martin Luther, Jr. "I Have a Dream." In *A Testament of Hope: The Essential Writings and Speeches of Martin Luther King, Jr.,* edited by James M. Washington, 217–20. San Francisco: HarperSanFrancisco, 1992.

Labberton, Mark. *Called: The Crisis and Promise of Following Jesus Today.* Downers Grove, IL: InterVarsity, 2014.

Lee, Ahmi. *Preaching God's Grand Drama: A Biblical-Theological Approach.* Grand Rapids: Baker Academic, 2019.

Levertov, Denise. "Beginners." In *Candles in Babylon,* 82. New York: New Directions, 1978.

Linn, Dennis, and Sheila Fabricant Linn. *Sleeping with Bread: Holding What Gives You Life.* Mahwah, NJ: Paulist, 1994.

Lischer, Richard. *Just Tell the Truth: A Call to Faith, Hope, and Courage.* Grand Rapids: Eerdmans, 2021.

———. "Preaching and the Rhetoric of Promise." *Word and World* 8.1 (1988) 66–79.

Long, Thomas. "Preaching God's Future: The Eschatological Context of Christian Proclamation." In *Sharing Heaven's Music: The Heart of Christian Preaching: Essays in Honor of James Earl Massey,* edited by Barry L. Callen, 191–201. Nashville: Abingdon, 1995.

———. *Testimony: Talking Ourselves into Being Christian.* San Francisco: Jossey-Bass, 2004.

———. *The Witness of Preaching.* 2nd ed. Louisville: Westminster John Knox, 2005.

Long, Thomas, and Cornelius Plantinga. *A Chorus of Witnesses: Model Sermons for Yesterday's Preacher.* Grand Rapids: Eerdmans, 1994.

Bibliography

Lundblad, Barbara K. *Marking Time: Preaching Biblical Stories in Present Tense.* Nashville: Abingdon, 2007.

Luther, Martin. "The Babylonian Captivity of the Church." In *Luther's Works,* vol. 3, edited by Jaroslave Pelikan and Helmut T. Lehmann, 3–126. Philadelphia: Fortress, 1955–1976.

McGrath, Alister. *The Christian Theology Reader.* Malden, MA: Wiley Blackwell, 2017.

McKenzie, Alyce. *Hear and Be Wise: Becoming a Preacher and Teacher of Wisdom.* Nashville: Abingdon, 2004.

———. *Making a Scene in the Pulpit: Vivid Preaching for Visual Listeners.* Louisville: Westminster John Knox, 2018.

———. *Novel Preaching.* Louisville: Westminster John Knox, 2010.

Milton, John. *Paradise Lost.* Oxford: Oxford University Press, 2005.

Moltmann, Jürgen. *Theology of Hope.* New York: Harper & Row, 1967.

Moss, Otis, III. *Blue Note Preaching in a Post-Soul World.* Louisville: Westminster John Knox, 2015.

Norris, Kathleen. *Amazing Grace: A Vocabulary of Faith.* New York: Riverhead, 1998.

Oliver, Mary. "Sometimes." In *Devotions: The Selected Poems of Mary Oliver,* 104–6. New York: Penguin, 2017.

Ortlund, Dane. *Gentle and Lowly: The Heart of Christ for Sinners and Sufferers.* Wheaton, IL: Crossway, 2020.

Pasquarello, Michael. *We Speak Because We Have First Been Spoken.* Grand Rapids: Eerdmans, 2009.

Peterson, Eugene. *Five Smooth Stones for Pastoral Work.* Grand Rapids: Eerdmans, 1992.

———. *Under the Unpredictable Plant.* Grand Rapids: Eerdmans, 1992.

Peterson, Jordan B. *12 Rules for Life: An Antidote to Chaos.* New York: Random House, 2018.

Pieper, Josef. *Faith, Hope, and Love.* San Francisco: Ignatius, 1986.

Powell, Kara, and Stephen Argue. *Growing With: Every Parent's Guide to Helping Teenagers and Young Adults Thrive in Their Faith, Family, and Future.* Grand Rapids: Baker, 2019.

Powery, Luke A. *Dem Dry Bones: Preaching, Death, and Hope.* Minneapolis: Fortress, 2012.

Radbertus, Paschasius. *De Fe, Spe, et Charitie.* In *Thesaurus Anecdotorum Novissimus: Seu Vererum Momumentorum.* Augsburg: Veith, 1729.

Redpath, Alan. "Thinking Upon Jesus." *Deeper Christian,* https://deeperchristian.com/thinking-upon-jesus-alan-redpath/.

Schmit, Clayton. *Sent and Gathered: A Worship Manual for the Missional Church.* Grand Rapids: Baker Academic, 2009.

Smith, James K. A. *You Are What You Love: The Spiritual Power of Habit.* Grand Rapids: Brazos, 2016.

Smith, Robert, Jr. "Preaching as a Contemplative Theological Task." In *Our Sufficiency Is of God: Essays on Preaching in Honor of Gardner C. Taylor,* edited by Timothy George, James Earl Massey, and Robert Smith Jr., 151–70. Macon, GA: Mercer University Press, 2010.

Snyder, Noel. *Sermons that Sing: Music and the Practice of Preaching.* Downers Grove, IL: IVP Academic, 2021.

Stanley, Andy. *Visioneering.* Sisters, OR: Multnomah, 1999.

Bibliography

Stanley, Andy, and Lane Jones. *Communicating for a Change*. Portland, OR: Multnomah, 2006.

Taleb, Nassim. *Antifragile: Things that Gain from Disorder*. New York: Penguin, 2012.

Taylor, Barbara Brown. *An Altar in the World*. New York: HarperCollins, 2010.

———. "Beginning at the End." In *Chorus of Witnesses: Model Sermons for Today's Preacher*, 12–21. Grand Rapids: Eerdmans, 1994.

———. "Bothering God." In *Birthing the Sermon: Women Preachers on the Creative Process*, edited by Jana Childers, 153–68. St. Louis: Chalice, 2001.

———. *The Preaching Life*. Lanham, MD: Rowman and Littlefield, 1993.

Thomas, Frank. *Exodus Preaching: Crafting Sermons about Justice and Hope*. Nashville: Abingdon, 2018.

Thompson, Bard. "The Reformed Church in the Palatinate." In *Essays on the Heidelberg Catechism*, by Bard Thompson et al., 31–52. Philadelphia: United Church, 1963.

Wells, Samuel. "Teaching Eucharist." A sermon preached in the Duke University Chapel, September 20, 2009.

White, William. *Fatal Attractions: Sermons on the Seven Deadly Sins*. Nashville: Abingdon, 1992.

Willard, Dallas. "Live Life to the Full." *Christian Herald*, October 14, 2001. https://dwillard.org/articles/live-life-to-the-full.

Williams, Rowan. *Being Disciples: Essentials of the Christian Life*. London: SPCK, 2016.

Wong, Hosanna. "I Will Not Be Afraid." Sermon preached at Eastlake Church, Chula Vista, CA, October 9, 2018. https://www.youtube.com/watch?v=QCOpy9h_cao.

Wright, N. T. *Simply Good News: Why the Gospel Is News and What Makes it Good*. New York: HarperCollins, 2014.

www.ingramcontent.com/pod-product-compliance
Lightning Source LLC
Chambersburg PA
CBHW022121160426
43197CB00009B/1115